1995

PLANNING A SUCCESSFUL CONFERENCE

SURVIVAL SKILLS FOR SCHOLARS

Managing Editor: Mitchell Allen

Survival Skills for Scholars provides you, the professor or advanced graduate student working in a college or university setting, with practical suggestions for making the most of your academic career. These brief, readable guides will help you with skills that you are required to master as a college professor but may have never been taught in graduate school. Using hands-on, jargon-free advice and examples, forms, lists, and suggestions for additional resources, experts on different aspects of academic life give invaluable tips on managing the day-to-day tasks of academia—effectively and efficiently.

Volumes in This Series

SURVIVAL SKILLS FOR SCHOLARS

PLANNING A SUCCESSFUL CONFERENCE

CYNTHIA WINTER

SAGE Publications
International Educational and Professional Publisher
Thousand Oaks   London   New Delhi

The checklist format at the beginning of each chapter was inspired by *The CLC Manual*. This and other material from *The CLC Manual* is reprinted with permission of the Convention Liaison Council, Washington, DC.

For information address:

SAGE Publications, Inc.
2455 Teller Road
Thousand Oaks, California 91320

SAGE Publications Ltd.
6 Bonhill Street
London EC2A 4PU
United Kingdom

SAGE Publications India Pvt. Ltd.
M-32 Market
Greater Kailash I
New Delhi 110 048 India

Printed in the United States of America

Library of Congress Cataloging-in-Publication Data

Winter, Cynthia.
    Planning a successful conference / author, Cynthia Winter.
        p. cm. — (Survival skills for scholars ; v. 13)
    Includes bibliographical references.
    ISBN 0-8039-5524-3. — ISBN 0-8039-5525-1 (pbk.)
    1. Forums (Discussion and debate)—Planning. 2. Universities and colleges—Faculty—Congresses—Planning. I. Title. II. Series.
LC6519.W56 1994
808.53—dc20   94-15526
                                                                    CIP

94 95 96 97 98 10 9 8 7 6 5 4 3 2 1

Sage Production Editor: Yvonne Könneker

Contents

Preface

You have just been asked by your dean to be in charge of a
1 ½ day conference. This is something you have never done
before, and you do not really know where to begin. This book
is designed to guide you through each stage—from the beginning panic to the successful finish when you put up your
feet, relax, and feel good about a job well-done.

In the past, many universities had paid convention planning staff at their disposal, and it was relatively easy for the
planner. Now with budget cutbacks, meeting chairs often must
do most of the work themselves: sign contracts for speakers
and facilities; prepare a budget; plan the program; market the
meeting; work with facility staff in room setups, catering,
audiovisual requirements; process registrations, and so on.

I have been planning academic conferences for over 25 years
for the National Council on Family Relations (NCFR), a nonprofit educational association serving family professionals.
Over 70% of its members are in the academic field. I am also
a certified meeting professional through the Convention Liaison Council. The majority of this book's content is based on
personal experience and countless meetings with other planners, hotel personnel, and travel agencies.

Professional meetings have changed dramatically in the
last decade. In planning conferences, it is necessary to learn
from both good and bad experiences of previous meetings.

The days of the "handshake" between a university or association and the meeting place are gone. Today, planning a successful meeting is a partnership of the planning committee, the facility staff, and the attendees. Together they must cooperate to achieve a meeting that is beneficial to everyone. Today's attendees are also different from those 25 years ago. They view continuing education as a means to a richer and fuller professional life.

Through the years I have learned that there are four basic rules in planning professional meetings:

Planning Rules

- Put everything in writing.
- Be flexible.
- Plan thoroughly.
- Expect the unexpected.

These rules will be helpful for all involved in the partnership of a successful meeting. It is best to have everything well documented, allowing for fewer misunderstandings among all parties, but one must also be realistic when it comes to planning.

- No meeting facility will meet 100% of your needs; facilities are designed for multiple purposes.
- Speakers can change their minds at the last minute.
- Attendance may be smaller or larger than anticipated.

Recently, I coordinated a convention for 1,000 people in Minneapolis. It featured simultaneous programs for adults, children, and teenagers. Attendance had increased by over 200 after the hotel contract had been signed. I was apprehensive because I knew the facilities would be stretched to the limit. On the opening day, one of the attendees approached me and said, "Good luck! We've had our teachers' conventions here, and this hotel has been ghastly! We finally moved to another hotel because they did such a bad job."

One month before the convention, I had sent the hotel our staging guide with specific directions on room setups and other details. The hotel staff did a beautiful job, going above the call of duty to see to the needs of all people.

On the last day, this same attendee said, "I can't believe this. They were fantastic! You must have done a great job of planning. This is much different than our previous experiences here." It pays to plan!

Small and Large Meetings

Similarities and differences between small and large meetings need to be examined. I define a small meeting as a 1- to 2-day program with fewer than 200 attendees. A large meeting is 3 to 6 days with a complex program and more than 200 attendees. Much of the planning is the same for both small and large meetings, but the amount of work and the process will be different.

First, let us look at some similarities: It is necessary to select a location and to sign a contract with the facility. Even if your university has a conference center, you will need to sign a contract. You also must decide if you will provide lodging for the attendees, and if so, where? If you have food functions scheduled, it is necessary to send catering guarantees to the facility. Finally, you must schedule a program.

Now let us compare the differences:

Small Meetings	*Large Meetings*
Generally, meeting participants have materials sent to them for advance preparation.	Materials are not sent in advance of the conference.
Usually, the audience is more specialized, and there is more group participation.	The larger audience will be more diverse, and there is less group participation.
The meeting is probably focused on one specific topic. Fewer presentations are given, and fewer slots are scheduled for several small, concurrent sessions.	The meeting may have an overall theme, but there are a variety of sessions covering many different topics. Many breakout sessions will be scheduled throughout the conference.
Registration costs will generally be lower; it will take less time to process registrations.	Registration costs will be higher; it will take more time to process registrations.
There will be fewer activities to plan during the meeting.	There will be many concurrent activities throughout the conference.
There is a greater likelihood that inexperienced people will handle meeting details. Fewer people will work on logistical details.	Generally, people handling the meeting details need to be more experienced in conference planning. Many people will be involved in all aspects of the planning.

What Is in This Book

Each chapter describes a step in the meeting planning process. Generally, chapters follow a chronological order, although many steps will be concurrent, from early planning through execution of the meeting. There is a checklist at the beginning of each chapter, followed by explanations. One key to good planning is knowing the right questions to ask those who are providing services to your meeting. I will give you a list of questions to ask in each of these situations. At the end of the book I will list supplementary materials: a sample site prospectus, a page from a staging guide with instructions to meeting facility staff, and additional resources such as meeting planning periodicals to which you may subscribe and books on meeting planning.

It is important that planners pay attention to attendees' needs when planning a conference. The first chapter is devoted to learning about professional conferences and meetings from an attendee's perspective. To be an effective teacher and researcher it is crucial to keep up with the latest research trends and teaching techniques. Tips on maximizing learning and advice on making valuable contacts will be shared.

You will learn about the stages of planning a conference: designing a meeting (who, what, when, where, why), selecting a site and planning a budget so that you know how much to charge for registration, planning the program schedule, marketing your meeting, preparing for the meeting (the more advance work you do will make your job easier on site), setting up on-site logistics during the meeting (conferring with facility staff, speaker needs, registration, etc.), and organizing postmeeting activities (shipping materials and conducting evaluations).

I consider meeting planning a giant puzzle. There are many pieces to the process. As you plan, the pieces fit together to make a complete picture, and you gain a lot of satisfaction from a job well-done. Good luck as you plan your meeting!

Acknowledgments

This book would not have been possible without the help of many people. Truly "no man (or woman) is an island."

I would like to thank my husband, Douglas Winter, for standing beside me in this project. His unfailing encouragement and love helped me realize that I could write the book. I have learned a lot from him throughout our marriage. This book would not have been possible without him.

The next person to whom I owe a debt of gratitude is Dr. Mary Jo Czaplewski, executive director of the National Council on Family Relations. She has guided and encouraged the staff to "reach for the stars" and grow professionally. Because of this I attended workshops, joined professional associations, and became a Certified Meeting Professional. She helped in the initial editing of the book and made helpful suggestions for improvement.

Thanks to my brother, Dr. Neil Leroux, an assistant professor of speech communication at the University of Minnesota, Morris, one of the chief proofreaders of the manuscript. He gave great assistance in the writing style.

Thanks to Kathy Collins Royce and Sonja Almlie, NCFR staff, who also helped in the proofing and gave content assistance.

I want to thank the reviewers of this book: John Sherry, Ph.D, J.L. Kellogg Graduate School of Management, Northwestern University; Janet Astner, meeting services manager,

American Sociological Association; Jill Cohen Kolb, M.A., Family Sexual Abuse Treatment, Inc.; and Fred Williams, AEJMC, University of South Carolina, Columbia. They gave many helpful suggestions in the direction of the book. Thanks to Dr. DeWayne Woodring, executive director of the Religious Conference Management Association and chairman of the Convention Liaison Council, who reviewed the content of the book.

There are others who have stood beside me and guided me as I matured through the years. These include my parents, Mary Ruth Turner and the late Richard Leroux; and Ruth Adams, Mary Lou Anderson, and Ruth Jewson, who worked with me at NCFR for many years.

I wish to thank the following people who assisted me with the content of chapter 1: Karen Blaisure, Joan Comeau, Mary Jo Czaplewski, William Doherty, Margaret Feldman, Marilyn Flick, Lori Kaplan, Neil Leroux, Michael Sporakowski, and David Wright.

I want to especially thank Mitch Allen of Sage Publications for asking me to write the book. This was something I never dreamed was possible, but he kept insisting that I could do it. I am grateful he convinced me! This was a tremendous learning experience, and I gained far more than I will ever be able to give to others.

1 | Getting the Most From a Professional Conference

Checklist 1.1

☐ Learn about the benefits of conference attendance.
☐ Submit a proposal for presentation at the convention.
☐ Prepare your presentation if you are on the program.
☐ Plan ahead before you leave for the conference.
☐ Promote yourself at the meeting job service.
☐ Be an active participant in conference activities.
☐ Share your meeting experiences with your colleagues back home.

A conference is successful only if there are attendees. The most carefully planned, beautifully orchestrated meeting will be a dismal failure if no one shows up to hear the speakers. This chapter discusses the convention from the perspective of the attendees. Conference planners must constantly put themselves in the attendees' shoes and develop a program to meet their needs.

Learn About the Benefits
of Conference Attendance

1. Keeping up.

The academic world expects everyone in the teaching profession to keep up with the latest research and developments in their fields to offer fresh approaches to their students. One of the most exciting ways to do this is to attend professional meetings. Conferences provide up-to-the-minute information and opportunities to become actively involved. Well-known leaders give keynote addresses on their topics of expertise. Many other professionals and graduate students also present their work, much of it new research or work in progress. Several years ago, a graduate student told me, "The money I spent this week was worth every penny! I learned so much at this conference. It was a good supplement to my full semester at school."

The next four benefits will be discussed later in this chapter.

2. Advancing your career by presenting in sessions.
3. Becoming involved in your professional association's activities.
4. Meeting new people and renewing acquaintances.
5. Checking out new publications at the exhibits.

Submit a Proposal
for Presentation at the Convention

Presenting a paper at a conference is a step toward becoming more involved in the sponsoring association. It is a good way to get to know people. Some academic associations solicit paper submissions that are blind-reviewed, so that everyone has the same chance for acceptance. Many educational institutions provide travel funds only to those presenting at a conference. Therefore, it is important to submit a proposal. If you are hesitant about submitting one by yourself, ask a colleague to work with you on a project and submit it jointly. If the proposal is accepted and you present at the conference, you will be recognized by your peers. Leaders in your field may be in the audience. You will receive feedback on your work, which will help you learn about your strengths and weaknesses.

Tips for Submitting a Proposal

- Contact the sponsoring organization and ask for an instruction kit and forms. If you have questions, ask colleagues or members of the program committee.
- Follow the instructions explicitly. Be sure to send all the necessary items and submit everything by the stated deadline. In some organizations, proposals are immediately rejected if the instructions have not been followed.
- If the proposals are to be blind-reviewed, do not put the authors' names and addresses on the title page. Also, do not refer to the authors' names within the text. To blind-review means that the reviewers judge proposals according to standardized criteria without knowing the authors' identities.
- If you prepare a proposal that lends itself to several types of formats, you may have a better chance of acceptance. In most professional conferences all formats are considered equal in merit. The National Council on Family Relations (NCFR) strives to offer a balanced program using many formats, yet over 60% of the people who submit list "papers" as their first choice. Papers account for only 35% of NCFR's program: Some authors will need to present in alternative formats, or they will be rejected because of space limitations.

Prepare Your Presentation
if You Are on the Program

If your proposal is accepted and you are on the program at the conference, be fully prepared. Your presentation will leave a first impression of your work. If it is positive, your colleagues will have a good overall impression of you, and your work is reinforced.

Preparing an Oral Presentation

- An oral presentation should take no more than 15 minutes. A rule of thumb is that 5 minutes of speaking time equals two to three pages of typed material. Remember that a paper delivered orally should be different in style from an article meant to be read in print. Use your printed paper as a source, and prepare an outline to use for your speech. Most attendees do not like to hear papers read; however, talking off the top of your head can also annoy them.

- When structuring your presentation, bring out the direction your research has taken. Emphasize the *results* and *interpretation* rather than techniques. Use the first few minutes to place the research in some historical and developmental context, and then present some practical applications of your work. Attendees want to hear both aspects when they attend a session.

- The critical times of your speech are the first 2 minutes and the last minute. Develop an excellent introduction and a stunning conclusion. Adhere to your time limit.

- Put your key points on overheads, slides, or flip charts. Use large type sizes on all visuals. There should be no more than six words per line and no more than six lines per page on a transparency or a slide. Here is a simple test to see if your lettering is large enough. Put the overhead on the floor; if you cannot read it standing up, the print is too small. Ask ahead of time if you will be close enough to the equipment to manipulate your own visuals. If it will be a distance from where you are speaking, you will need someone to assist you, and you will need to number the overheads or slides and mark on your speech outline where the visuals will be used.

- Talk to the session presider ahead of time about his or her expectations. Send a copy of your biographical material and the completed paper or abstract to the presider and the discussant.

- Try to practice your presentation before a small group of supportive colleagues to ensure an effective performance. Frank comments and acceptance of such comments are basic ingredients for a good presentation. Speech departments at some universities may offer help to novice speakers.

- Bring plenty of handout copies to the conference. The handout should summarize your main points and include implications or practical ideas for one to two areas of policy, practice, or education. Bring a clipboard and a sign-up sheet for names and addresses of those who want further information. If you run out of handouts, mail copies to those who request them. It might be a good idea to bring self-adhesive labels for individuals to address. This will save you time later on. Make sure you have the budget to do this.

Presenting Your Speech

- Arrive 15 to 20 minutes early to meet with the session presider, other presenters, and the discussant. If you ordered audio-visual equipment, be sure it is working.
- When speaking, assume that whatever catastrophes can happen will happen, and be flexible in preparing your speech. If catastrophes happen, use a little humor.
- Stay within the allotted time limit. Stop on time. Remember there are other speakers during the session. Be considerate of their time.
- When you speak, establish eye contact with the audience; vary your styles of presentation. Be enthusiastic. If you are not impassioned by your work, do not expect the audience to be.
- Enjoy yourself as you present your paper. Your audience will be more relaxed.
- Do not read the handouts verbatim when talking. Simply refer to them, but allow participants to be involved in developing the outcome.

Poster Presentation

A poster is a display format with a short abstract, headlines, charts, graphs, and other visual features. It allows opportunities for individual contact and in-depth discussion between presenters and attendees.

Tips for Preparing a Poster

- It is recommended that you use a computer and a laser printer with proportional type fonts. Graphics software (e.g., Harvard Graphics) can develop excellent graphs and diagrams. Hand drawings are out.
- Begin with a heading, in large type, that lists the title of your presentation and the names of the authors.
- All material in the poster should be self-explanatory and eye-catching; it should also communicate to the audience quickly. You have just a few seconds to "hook" an attendee's interest.
- Color can add emphasis effectively. Keep visual material simple and clear. Borders give your poster a polished look. Good-sized margins around the text and white space within the text are helpful to the reader. Frame each white sheet with a colored background.
- Minimize the amount of text. Only an abstract, an introduction or purpose, a description of method and/or sample, and conclusions are necessary. Use headings and labels. Bullets in text highlight points. The bulk of information should be presented in table, graph, or diagram format. Bear in mind that items on a poster should be large enough to be read from distances of 3 feet or more. Use the floor test to see if the poster is readable from a distance; if you cannot read it standing up, the print is too small.
- Do not mount illustrations on heavy board because it may be difficult to keep them in position on the poster board.
- Have plenty of copies of a simple abstract and a sign-up sheet for those who want to receive the complete paper.

At the Conference

- Plan to arrive 15 to 20 minutes before the scheduled poster time. Check to see where your poster is to be set up.
- Bring pushpins, staples, or Velcro to fasten your material to the poster board.
- Be prepared to talk in-depth about your presentation. Invite discussion and networking by asking attendees questions.

Listen to their responses and tailor your comments about your poster to their interests.

Round Tables

Round table sessions use a discussion format and are usually limited to 10 people, including the presenter.

- Give an overview of your topic during the first 15 to 20 minutes.
- After the overview, engage the group in discussion. Have questions prepared in advance to ensure that everyone has an opportunity to discuss the topic. This is the chance for people who have followed your work to discuss it with you on a more personal level. Do not read your handouts verbatim. You may refer to them, but allow the group to engage in discussion.

Session Presider

- Read the biographical material sent from each presenter and review the papers or abstracts before the session.
- Arrive 15 to 20 minutes before the session begins to meet with the presenters.
- Begin the session on time even if people are still arriving.
- Introduce each speaker and the topic. Be concise. The introductions should take no more than 5 minutes.
- Monitor the time flow. Be sure each speaker begins and ends promptly. Develop a signal process for speakers. Give all presenters an opportunity to speak before the discussion period begins.
- During the discussion period, be firm about time limits and protect the speakers from long-winded questions that may be orations of opinion. Help the speaker move on from them with humor and grace.
- End the session on time.

Discussant

- Obtain the addresses and phone numbers of the presenters so that you can talk with them about their papers. Read the papers and/or abstracts *before* the conference and be prepared with a concise summary.

- Summarize and critique each paper that has been presented. Try to find common themes ahead of time and be creative in integrating the papers. Add an interesting quote. Do not use this time to discuss your own work. Help the participants and the audience take some useful knowledge with them. Help them answer the question "What difference does this research make?"

Plan Ahead Before You Leave for the Conference

Review the Printed Program Carefully

- Read the conference materials *thoroughly* as soon as possible. This will help you take advantage of all events. Note all of the sessions you would like to attend, then begin to choose among them. Highlight your "must sees." Typically, you may find two or more sessions you would like to attend scheduled simultaneously. Sometimes a topic in a slightly altered form is discussed again elsewhere in the program.

- Write out your schedule on a separate sheet of paper. Rank the presentations you want to attend, then those you are willing to forego if another option becomes available (such as a newly scheduled presentation, a chance to meet with a leader in the field). Try to schedule association business and committee meetings and receptions and/or parties. Be sure to include films you want to preview and appointments you make.

Make Travel Arrangements and Seek Conference Funding

Traveling to a conference is an expensive investment. As soon as you decide to attend, begin calculating costs so that you are prepared to seek financial assistance. Travel funds are scarce in many universities, and it is important that you do your homework. Some agencies will send employees to a conference if they can be assured of receiving pragmatic materials. Other agencies will send someone who promises to return and offer an in-house training on a particular conference topic. Most universities will pay for travel only if you are on the program.

If you need to travel by air, contact an airline or travel agency. Check the registration material to see if there is a designated airline with discounted convention rates. Ask for a schedule and fares, but do not make a reservation before you talk to your administrator. If you are using a travel agent, ask about the cost of ground transportation (shuttle service between the airport and the conference facility) or car rentals.

Prepare the following information to give to your administrator:

- Describe the event: theme, major speakers, session titles, paper titles, and so on. Leave a marked copy of the conference mailing piece or program with the particular sessions you would like to attend.
- Tell about your role at the conference. Are you going as an attendee? Are you presenting? How will it help your research? Will this enhance your course work? Are you a member of a committee that will be meeting during the conference?
- Itemize your projected expenses: registration fee, travel, lodging, ground transportation, preconference workshop fees, continuing education fee, and mileage and parking fees if you are driving.
- Plan the type of follow-up you will give to the administrator following the conference.

After your travel funds have been approved, ask the administrator what forms are required and what receipts must be saved. Find out if the university pays directly for the airline ticket or if you must purchase it first and then turn in the bill for reimbursement.

Graduate students who want to attend a conference should check about available funds at the sponsored programs office in the graduate school. They should also ask the sponsoring organization of the conference about available scholarships. They can then meet with the administrator to see what support is available from the department.

Try to make airline reservations during fare wars when rates are low. Make reservations for sleeping rooms at the conference facility as soon as possible. Most conferences reserve a block of rooms that are guaranteed up to a cutoff date. If the attendance is larger than anticipated, the room block may fill before the cutoff date, and those who call at the last minute will be forced to stay elsewhere. Guarantee your first night's reservation with a credit card, if you will be arriving late.

When you are at the conference, keep a running record of meals and expenses. Trying to remember these later is difficult. Ask the conference sponsor to identify expenses by category in its receipt. Be sure to keep receipts for meals, lodging, ground transportation, registration, and so on. Turn them in to your administrator after you return, or keep them to use as possible tax deduction receipts.

Make Networking Plans

- Ask your colleagues to introduce you to people you want to meet. Perhaps you can schedule a time when you can all get together for discussion.
- When you are reviewing the program, make an hourly schedule, including the mealtimes you are available. Then write down the names of people you would like to meet, and call or write to them before the conference to make an appointment.
- After you have noted the people you want to meet, read some of their books and articles. It will be easier to converse with them if you are somewhat familiar with their work.
- Bring your return address labels or print your name and address on a sheet of labels that can be peeled off, so that you can quickly attach these labels to any sign-up lists.
- Bring along business cards to hand to exhibitors, presenters, and new friends.

- Some conferences ask for student volunteers to help with running the event. Usually, the registration fee is refunded in exchange for working a certain number of hours. It is a good way to meet people and to learn about how conferences are run. Many student aides at NCFR conferences have become active in our association. If you work in the registration area or job service, you may meet some of the leaders in the field.

Miscellaneous Notes

- Leave the name and telephone number of the facility with your family and colleagues. Also give the phone number of the meeting sponsor (usually, organizers will have a central station at the property where phone calls can be taken). Give your schedule to your family and colleagues so that if an emergency arises it will be easier for conference staff to find you.
- Remember the image you want to project at the conference as you pack your clothes. This is particularly important if you will be using the job service. Find out if the hotel has exercise equipment, a pool, or other facilities, and pack what you need.
- Bring clothes for all types of weather. Recently, my executive director and I traveled to North Carolina for a site visit. We had been told that the temperature would be in the 50° to 60° range, and we were ready for that type of weather. On the second day of our trip, there was a blizzard with a below-zero windchill.
- Leave space in your luggage for copies of papers, books, flyers, and other information.

Promote Yourself at the Meeting Job Service

Many conferences offer on-site job services. For most universities and colleges, this is a major place for initial interviews. It is cost-effective because there are no additional expenses for the interview. Employment services provide job opening lists and candidate files and provide a space for preliminary interviews. You may also meet prospective employers in sessions in addition to the interview.

Tips for Using the Employment Service

- Write or phone the conference sponsors and ask for instructions and forms. Follow the directions explicitly when preparing your materials.
- Bring plenty of résumés and business cards with you. You may find out about openings in addition to the ones listed in the job service. If possible, send your material before the conference so that you are listed in the initial files. Let colleagues know that you are looking for a job so that they can give your name to employers.
- Be assertive when you are at the conference. Register at the job service when it opens and keep coming back because, frequently, new jobs are listed. Usually, there is a message board for candidates and employers. Leave messages for those you would like to contact and keep checking. If there is no response to your notes, try leaving a message in their rooms or ask colleagues to help find them, but keep trying! There are more people trying to find jobs than there are job openings, so you must be vigilant.
- Remember that you are making an impression at all conference events: sessions, receptions, and parties. Network, dress, and conduct yourself appropriately. Send thank-you notes to all persons who gave you an interview.

Be an Active Participant in Conference Activities

Catch the Intellectual Highlights

- Attend all main sessions. Usually, these speakers are well-known and give interesting talks.
- If you are attending with a group of people, examine which presentations each of you would like to attend. Go to different presentations so that you can cover more topics, and share information and handouts later.
- Take notes during the sessions. As you listen, try to think of how the presentations can apply to your own work.

- Attend all types of sessions: posters, papers, and round tables. Each type of session offers unique ways of learning and networking. Go to small informal sessions where there are opportunities for interaction between presenters and the audience.
- Stay after sessions and introduce yourself to the speakers. Be courteous of their time.
- Some sessions offer three or four papers, only one of which is of interest to you. Conference etiquette allows for you to quietly enter or leave a session between papers. If two presentations you would like to attend are scheduled at the same time, leave a message for the author so that you can get a copy of the handout, or contact him or her after the conference.
- During a session, think about the kinds of questions you may want to ask the speaker during the question-and-answer period. Be sure to ask questions. It opens the door for networking later. Do not ask a question that gives the impression you were not listening. If you just caught a thought, ask, "Could you clarify?" Frame a question, for example, "Have you worked on this in any other way?"; "Are you doing other work dealing with this topic?" Keep questions brief, and do not seize the stage for yourself and refer to your own work.

Integrate Yourself Into the Association

- Membership in professional associations is a way of advancing your career and an excellent way to network. Many of the people who are active in associations and attend conferences are leaders in their fields. If you become active in the association, you will be able to work with them. In many associations you must belong to the organization to present at the conference or submit a journal article, both of which are necessary for tenure.
- Attend business or committee meetings. If you see some that you are interested in, ask if they are open meetings and if you can attend. You may be able to offer input and discover ways of becoming active in the organization. Often the best contacts are in these meetings. Most organizations have smaller committees or sections. Usually, people who are active in these groups become better known and later can move to leadership positions.

- Some associations need members to give volunteer service to function effectively. This can also benefit you because you may be working side by side with officers and board members. Volunteer for all types of positions: Review journal or manuscript articles or conference proposals, be a presider or a recorder, work on a committee. Do not turn down any opportunities, even for mundane tasks. Think about how you can learn from the experience. It may benefit you now and in the future.

Visit the Exhibits

Exhibits are an integral part of many professional meetings. Professors are always looking for new material for their research and teaching. Visiting the exhibits provides one-stop shopping. Many publishers sell by mail, and this is your only chance to look at their materials before buying. Most publishers who are at a conference display their newest materials or introduce new ones. An added perk is that you may meet the authors face-to-face.

Check the exhibitor listing carefully. At academic conferences there may be publishers, graduate schools, foundations, government agencies that offer grants, computer software companies, and other companies offering services for academics. This is a chance for you to check them out and save hours of phone calls at a later date.

Exhibits also offer places for you to meet publishers face-to-face. They take very seriously the contacts and conversations at the conferences. If you have ideas for a book, take copies of the outline with you and make an appointment to meet with the acquisitions editor or other publisher representative. Ask for an informational interview to determine the requirements for submitting a prospectus.

Exhibits are also good places to meet people and to try out your networking skills. It is easy to initiate a conversation while looking at the books.

Pick up brochures and catalogues as you go through the exhibits and study them while you are at the conference. Go back to the booth and try to order what you want while you are there. Find out if the exhibitor plans to sell materials at reduced prices at the end of the conference.

Take Advantage of Networking Opportunities

Conferences are great places to meet new colleagues and see old friends. The interaction in sessions and during breaks is often as valuable as the presentations. You never know when you will meet someone who is doing work similar to yours who can give you fresh insights. You also have important views that can help other colleagues.

Some tips to help you become more comfortable in networking are listed below.

- Attend special sessions for new meeting participants. You can learn strategies for negotiating the sessions and tips on figuring out which sessions you should attend. You can introduce yourself to other first-time attendees who might be there alone also. A few years ago, I attended a conference of meeting planners, and I did not know anyone when I arrived. At the newcomers' orientation, I met another woman who was also attending for the first time. We decided to room together to save money and we got to be good friends. We now room together each year when we attend that conference. If I had not gone to the orientation, I might never have met her.
- Check name badges. Many times they are coded according to who is a presenter, a student, or a new conference attendee. Watch for other people who are there for the first time and introduce yourself. Suggest meeting for a snack or a meal.
- Be assertive. Introduce yourself to everyone you meet in the hallway. Have a brief 3- to 5-second explanation of the kind of work you do to help break the ice. One professor introduces her students to colleagues at the beginning of the week, but then says, "Don't hang around me, go out on your own and meet people."
- Try to arrange some time when you can meet other people for a meal. Meeting people between sessions does not accomplish

as much because everyone is in a hurry to get somewhere. If you have contacted colleagues before the conference, meet at a central location such as registration so that it is easier to find each other.

- If you want to find someone, leave a message in several places, for example, on the conference message board; with the front desk at the facility; or, if you know the person's room number, slide a note under the door.

- Attend receptions and parties, especially those sponsored by college departments. Initiate a conversation. Do not wait for someone to talk to you. It may be easier to talk in the relaxed atmosphere of these functions.

- Spend time sitting in the central areas with colleagues. This is a great place for people you know to introduce you to people they know.

- Exchange business cards after meeting new colleagues. Make notes on the back so that you will not forget about their significance after the conference. Be sure to follow up with phone calls after you return home. This reinforces your contacts.

- Staying with a group of people you know can add to the fun and lower expenses. If you want to room with someone, but have no roommate, take advantage of offers to match you with another attender. It has been my experience that, if roommates are compatible, they can become good contacts for each other throughout the year.

Keep Physically Fit, Mentally Alert, and Safe

- Make sure you get enough rest *before* going to a conference and once you are there. Fatigue is predictable due to a combination of late evenings of presentations, dinners, or parties, and early sessions and business meetings.

- Do not skip meals and try to eat a balanced diet. You will feel better and get more out of the sessions.

- Take workout gear. Many conference facilities have indoor exercise equipment. Taking a break at some point during the day to exercise or walk can increase your energy level and prevent your feet from swelling after sitting for hours.

- Violence is present in every part of the country, and it is wise to take a few steps to be safe while at the conference: (a) Do not wear your convention badge outside the conference facility, making it obvious that you are a visitor; (b) stay in groups when walking outdoors; (c) use only unmarked rental cars; (d) when you are in your room, keep the door locked and the deadbolt engaged at all times; (e) if someone comes to your door, use the peephole to see who it is. Call the front desk or security if the person says that he or she is on the facility staff to see if this is correct and the visit is authorized; (f) be careful when riding an elevator by yourself; (g) leave valuables in a safe-deposit box.

Keep in Touch With Your Family and Colleagues While You Are Gone

If your meeting has a bulletin board, frequently check for messages. Call the front desk for phone calls.

Share Your Meeting Experience With Your Colleagues Back Home

- Purchase audio- and videotapes for sessions you *really* wanted to attend, but missed. For example, you can play the tapes while you commute or use them in your classes.
- After the conference, write up a summary of the sessions, including applications, and share them with your colleagues. Talk about how the new discoveries can help you in your present situation.

These are the things that can help you make the most of your convention experience. For the meeting planner, if you can understand the perspective of the conference attendees, you can better plan a meeting. Chapter 2, "Designing a Meeting," will discuss how to determine the purpose, the goals, and the objectives for your meeting and how to begin planning a basic program structure.

2 | Designing a Meeting

Checklist 2.1

☐ Determine the real purpose, goals, and objectives for your meeting.
☐ Research the needs and tastes of your audience.
☐ Set formats for the meeting and define roles of speakers, facilitators, and discussants.
☐ Plan the program committee structure, develop job descriptions, and build a working calendar.
☐ Select speakers and entertainment.
☐ Negotiate and draw up contracts with conference staff.

The success of conventions depends very little on such mundane matters as scheduling of seminars and expositions. It's content that holds people at conventions and that brings them back next year. . . . What confuses (and angers) them the most is not getting what they paid for—information.

—Conlin (1993)

Chapter 1 discussed the conference from the attendee's perspective. With this background it is now easier to begin planning. This chapter gives a broad overview of the planning process. Subsequent chapters will discuss the steps in detail.

Determine Purpose, Goals, and Objectives of the Conference

The first step is to write down the following vital information:

1. *Purpose, goals, and objectives of the conference.* For a small meeting you may have a specific topic to discuss, and the goal will be evident. If you are planning a larger meeting, there are several purposes for getting together: information, networking, resource seeking, scheduling small committee and business meetings of the sponsoring organization, job hunting, making money, a chance to see old friends. One of the important needs for some people in the 1990s is continuing education credit (CEC). When you define the purpose, the goals, and the objectives, it might be wise to consider whether CECs can be granted.[1]

We learned in chapter 1 that one secret to a successful educational meeting is to discover the real needs and interests of attendees. Try to uncover their priority issues and true concerns. There are several ways to do this; process these as you would do any other kind of research:

- Focus group interviews.
- Survey questionnaires.
- Sampling: Pretest a small percentage of the prospective audience with questions to help determine directions for future programming.

Once you have determined the interests of your prospective audience, synthesize the information into a set of definite

19

objectives for the meeting. Determine the real mission of the meeting. Decide what knowledge you are trying to share. Set specific objectives that can be measured.

2. *Who will be the conference attendees?* At the beginning stages of conference planning, deciding who should attend the conference determines the focus of your program and simplifies marketing strategies.

As you decide about your prospective attendees, ask yourself some questions:

- Will the audience be limited to academic attendees, mostly speakers, will it be open to the public, or will it include other professionals? If the people are primarily from the research community, the focus will undoubtedly be more research oriented. However, if educators attend, they may be looking for ideas to take back to their classrooms. Practitioners working in agencies will want practical ideas to use directly with their clients.

- What is the academic standing, the income bracket, and the lifestyle of your prospective audience? Are they graduate students with little money or professors who have more? If your attendees will be primarily university or association employed, it will be necessary to plan an intensive educational forum with very few luxuries. Most universities and associations have slashed funding for conferences, forcing attendees to pay a larger portion of expenses out of their own pockets. If your audience is highly subsidized for educational sessions, then you may be able to build in some special events.

3. *Date of event.* In setting the date, you must keep in mind airline fare restrictions, difficulties for faculty members taking time off, availability of the conference facility staff and speakers, and costs and restrictions of the conference facility.

4. *Name of event.* After planning the date, give the event a name. Decide on a central theme that is self-explanatory. This can be determined as you research the needs of the group and plan the program objectives.

5. *Coordinator of event.* A successful conference is a team effort, but it is necessary to name a coordinator who is respon-

sible for overseeing the entire event. Subcommittees will report to him or her. Meeting facility staff also prefer having one person with whom they can communicate. A clear line of communication helps avoid misunderstandings.

6. *Location of event.* For many academic conferences, the content is the most important part, but if the location is less than desirable, attendance may fall. If attendees have a miserable experience at the conference site, they may not return to other meetings that you offer. I can think of times when people were unhappy with the hotel where NCFR conferences were held, and I heard about it! Chapter 3 will discuss site selection.

Prepare a Checklist for Planning the Event

Planning an educational event takes a lot of effort, but the task becomes easier when you design a checklist and break everything into small, workable details. Use a three-ring binder. The following divisions are helpful:

- Calendar
- Purpose and site selection (includes prospectus sent to facilities and statistics from other meetings)
- Budget
- Committees
- Program
- Marketing
- Hotel staging guide and instructions
- Food and beverage
- Audiovisual equipment
- Exhibits
- Keynote speaker arrangements
- Staff schedules and instructions
- Speaker contracts
- Registration forms and lists

- Meeting minutes
- Miscellaneous (includes lists of materials needed at the conference site)

This information becomes your lifeline to the meeting. Several years ago, my staff and I were at the convention site early for preplanning. The fire alarm awoke us at 2:30 a.m. We began to plan our escape from our hotel, and the first thing I picked up was my conference notebook—even before my purse! Fortunately, it was a false alarm.

You will need to make a checklist at the beginning of each division in the notebook. The following information should be included on the first page of the notebook: name of event, date and place, purpose, goals, objectives, expected attendance, names, addresses, phone and fax numbers of committee chairs and members.

Each chapter in this book contains similar checklists for your notebook.

Select Planning Committees

If you are planning a small conference at a university, you may not have the luxury of a professional conference staff; the efforts of many people will be required. Once the general chair has been selected, you will need to choose your committees. It is important at the outset to develop a partnership. Each person on the planning committee has unique talents to contribute. The pooling of these resources always brings good results. Committees give the conference chair and staff valuable insights into the concerns and issues of the prospective attendees. Even though conference planning is a team effort, it is necessary to plan a committee structure so that all members will have a clear idea of responsibilities. One possible chain of command might be the following:

- General chair
- Program committee chair
- Local arrangements committee chair
- Subcommittee chairs
- Subcommittee members

Once you have determined the structure, you can start selecting the committees. In some associations, committee members are elected through the general membership. If this is not the case and you are selecting from volunteers, consider:

1. Reputation for professional expertise, executive-level responsibility, and professional standing are important. The people on the committee must be able to compromise with other committee members.
2. Look for diverse points of view, but choose those volunteers who are committed to putting the success of the conference above their own interests.
3. Choose people who are creative and willing to provide programs that will meet the needs of the prospective audience.
4. Compatibility is vital to a committee's success. The committee members will be working closely together for several months. The committee work is satisfying if the members have a common goal in mind. They will have an opportunity to have input into decisions that affect their profession (Ramsborg, 1992).

Next, write up job descriptions and duties of all committee members. When the tasks are completed, have committee members document specific steps to pass on to the next conference committee. When drafting the job descriptions, begin with a brief summary of the overall task, then write specific duties. For my own conferences, I have a handbook that includes a table of contents, working calendar of deadlines, general guidelines for all committee members, and specific job descriptions. See Appendix A for sample job descriptions.

Prepare a Working Calendar
for Planning Committees

After job descriptions are compiled, prepare a working calendar for all committee members. Deadlines are necessary for smoothly run conferences. Committee members have many demands with their own jobs, and it is easy to forget about conference duties. Providing a conference calendar enables members to weave it into their personal schedules. The best way to begin the calendar is to start with the conference itself and work backward.

The following calendar is an abbreviation of one the NCFR designed, based on an 18-month schedule. The conference has over 250 sessions and 600 to 700 presenters. If you are planning a smaller conference with just a few speakers and you have less time to plan, adapt your schedule and needs accordingly. If you are interested, you can contact me for a complete calendar.

Conference Calendar,
Conference Date: November 1993

18 months in advance
1. Initial meeting with those interested in being on the local arrangements committee.
2. Program chair selects conference theme.

14 months in advance
1. Select keynote speakers and mail speaker contracts.
2. Finalize local arrangements subcommittee chairs and members; give job descriptions.

12 months in advance
1. Program committee meets during the current conference.
2. Copy deadline for publicity news items.
3. Local arrangements committee meets during the conference for progress reports.
4. Send application form/instruction packet for the "Call for Proposals" to members and others interested.

11 months in advance

1. Compile and send evaluations from current conference to committee members.
2. Plenary speakers send biographical material, photo, and title of their presentation.

9 months in advance

1. Deadline for submitting conference proposals.
2. Local arrangements public relations committee prepares lists of prospective attendees to invite to the conference.
3. Send proposals that were submitted to the program committee for blind review.

7 months in advance

1. Program committee sends list of accepted proposals to the conference chair.
2. Local arrangements committee meets at the conference site.
3. Program committee meets to finalize program plans.

6 months in advance

1. Send letters of acceptance/rejection to all who submitted proposals.
2. Send major publicity material to prospective conference attendees' mailing list.

5 months in advance

1. Deadline for all changes for the printed conference program.

4 months in advance

1. Deadline for listing of award winners.
2. Prepare printed program and forms. Ad copy deadline.

3 months in advance

1. Mail printed program and registration materials.

2 months in advance

1. Deadline for requests of committee meeting times, audiovisual equipment, and menus.
2. Deadline for room arrangements for major speakers.
3. Compile and send audiovisual requests to the coordinator of the audiovisual equipment. Make arrangements to rent equipment.
4. Send initial press release to media contacts.

5. Compile and send travel schedule of keynote speakers to speaker arrangements committee.
6. Prepare signs for the conference.
7. Process conference registrations.

1 month in advance

1. Deadline for materials for registration packets.
2. Send staging guide and letter to facility.

3 weeks in advance

1. Deadline for early bird registration fees.
2. Deadline for all program changes for the program supplement.
3. Complete press kits and mail news releases about award winners.
4. Deadline for materials to be placed in the first-time attendees' packets.

2 weeks in advance

1. Prepare list of attendees, program supplement of changes, exhibit lists, and so on.
2. Prepare on-site registration packets.

10 days in advance

1. Print name badges for all registrants.
2. Prepare registration envelopes for each registrant (i.e., name badge, tickets, ribbons for special committees and board members).

1 week in advance

1. Generate a final computer registration list.

2 days in advance

1. Local arrangements committee meets.
2. Set up registration area, put out signs.
3. Meet with convention facility staff to go over the schedule.

Decide on the Conference Program Structure

Your program will determine the success of the conference. Again, remember to keep the needs of the attendees in mind as you plan. Chapter 3 will go into specific details about planning the schedule, but it is wise to write down an overall plan early so that you can decide on the types of speakers you want. You also need to have this basic program plan in place to know if the conference facility will accommodate you. These two pieces go hand in hand. For example, if you are using a facility at your university that offers limited breakout space, you will undoubtedly have to adjust your program schedule.

Make a Decision About Offering Exhibits

This must be decided early because you must schedule times for attendees to visit them. You need to send an invitation to prospective exhibitors several months in advance. You will also need meeting room space for exhibits in your meeting facility.

Plan Formats That
Are Exciting and Stimulating

"If the format looks boring to you on paper when you lay it out, chances are it will utterly stupefy your attendees" (Simmons, 1989b). Think about the following basic guidelines as you draw up an initial overall plan:

- Use your market research to decide on a theme and speakers that appeal to your potential audience.
- Try to incorporate the unique character and advantages of your facility and location into the meeting's format.

Construct a planning grid to help you look at the overall layout of the schedule. Chapter 3 has a sample program grid.

Select Speakers and Entertainment

You are now ready to plan the meat of the conference: speakers and entertainment. The first question is, Where can we find a good speaker? There are several ways to do this: (a) Check with regional speakers bureaus; and (b) for most universities, colleges, and professional associations, you will want to ask colleagues in the field and rely on your planning committee to find well-known speakers who have a vast knowledge of the subject you want to pursue.

As you review possible speakers, look back at the educational objectives of the conference. Will your prospective speaker's message be in tandem with the objectives? Ask the following questions when selecting speakers:

- Is the speaker a well-known expert on the topic? Is he or she respected in the field?
- Is the speaker an excellent public speaker? Is he or she interesting, humorous, persuasive? Has anyone on the committee or in the field heard the speaker? Will his or her presence stimulate attendance?
- Does the speaker have the ability to draw the audience into the presentation so that people in the audience feel like they are participating?
- Does the speaker have a solid research base on the topic?
- Will they make application of research to the topic?
- How much does the speaker charge?

It is a good idea to chart the strengths and weaknesses of each speaker so that the committee can decide which speakers will be best for your conference. After choosing the speakers, you are ready to contact them. The best way to begin is to phone the speaker or an agent, whichever is appropriate. Be prepared with a list of questions. Be specific. Include the date, the time, and the location of the conference; the conference theme; and a specific topic you wish to have the speaker address. Also include availability of the speaker, background about the conference and the audience, speaker fees, and expenses. Be up front.

After the speaker has agreed to come to your conference, confirm everything in writing. It is essential that speaker agreement forms be drawn up. See Appendix B for a sample speaker contract.

One other key to a successful conference is to *correspond periodically with the speakers*. Be sure to send them copies of all conference marketing materials.

Work With Conference Staff

Now that you have your conference designed, you are well on your way toward a successful meeting. If you are affiliated with a college or a university, there may be staff provided to help with some of the conference details. Some university conference centers provide services based on a sliding fee scale. These facilities may have staff to handle your registration, signs, meeting room, and catering arrangements if you are able to pay for it. Consider yourself fortunate if this is the case, because they can save you a great deal of time. Be sure to have *everything in writing* so that you and the staff are thinking alike.

Set up an initial meeting with the conference staff and the conference planning committee. Try to allow at least 2 to 3 hours so that both parties understand all arrangements. During this session the committee should give the staff a written conference plan. The staff can check over the plan and decide how they can best serve your needs.

Remember that the facility staff and the conference committee are a team. Discuss the following questions at your meeting:

- To whom should the conference facility staff report?
- Who is the key staff person to give period reports to the committee chair?
- What are the duties of *each* conference staff member?
- Who will be the key liaison with the facility and write up the staging guide?
- Who will write the publicity materials?

- Who will mail the publicity?
- Who will receive registrations, and how should checks be written?
- Who will print up signs?

Write up detailed job descriptions and set up a schedule for the conference staff to send written progress reports to the event chair. You may find it helpful to have forms devised for progress reports because the reports determine the next steps. Perhaps it may be necessary to change plans. For example, if registrations are lower than expected, the conference chair or committee may need to beef up the publicity campaign or cancel the event.

Check with the facility staff on costs. Key elements include the following:

- How are charges determined? Is there a flat fee for the entire event, or are you billed by the actual number of hours worked? Work out prices both ways.
- What are the estimated charges for each area of service?
- What is the estimated number of staff hours needed for each area of service?
- Is a down payment required?
- Are services to be paid for in advance? As a general rule, you should not pay the total bill before the conference. You should also request that all services be documented.
- Write a plan for *on-site* logistics at the conference. Determine the specific responsibilities of both the program committee and the facility staff. If the conference facility does not have staff to help you, or if it is too costly, you may need to use either existing office staff or volunteers to take care of the details.

If you take time to carefully plan at this stage of the conference, everything will run more smoothly.

This overview is just the beginning of the conference planning. The next step is selecting a site for your conference and preparing a budget. Chapter 3 will discuss these issues in detail.

Note

1. Every profession has different requirements for continuing education credits. Check your own bylaws, then investigate your industry's agencies or oversight authorities and appropriate governmental bodies. Items you will need to check for continuing education program accreditation include program selection, course approval criteria, specific learning objectives, credit reporting system, records processing, evaluation, and review of costs of producing and attending the sessions. Contact the Council on the Continuing Education Unit for more information. See Appendix K for their address.

3 | Site Selection and Budget

Checklist 3.1

☐ Develop specifications for the conference site, using conference objectives as a basis.
☐ Visit potential sites, doing a thorough site inspection.
☐ Negotiate a contract with the best conference facility, and get everything in writing!
☐ Plan a budget: Determine all conference expenses.
☐ Divide expenses by the anticipated number of attendees to determine registration costs.

You have now planned the goals and the objectives of your conference, you have selected the main speakers, and you are well on your way in planning the conference. The next step is choosing where you will meet. Site selection is crucial to the success of your meeting. Even if the meeting will be held on a campus, the right place for your event is both a science and an art. It is important for the program success as well as attendees' satisfaction. If the facility fits, participants will learn more and enjoy themselves more, and program leaders will be happier. Knowing more about selecting a site makes it easier to work with the faculty, the staff, and the employees of a facility.

If you are fortunate to have campus conference facilities at your disposal, you may be able to eliminate some of the steps described below, but always be sure to personally visit the facility. The list of steps in site selection is intended as a guideline in case you must hold the conference off-campus. Hotel general managers and sales reps have told me that they can do a much better job of hosting a conference when the meeting planners know what they want. If you know your group's needs, it is also easier to save money on the event. For example, some of the extras that facility managers may try to sell you are often unnecessary for a successful academic conference where the main goal is education.

I would like to briefly compare holding a conference in a university facility to a hotel or commercial conference center:

Box 3.1

University Conference Center	*Outside Facility*
Setting lends itself to a no frills, roll-up-your-sleeves learning experience. Meeting rooms are like classrooms designed for exchange of knowledge.	Extra facilities for recreation especially at a resort property. May be hard to concentrate with all the distractions. Some meeting rooms may not be as conducive to new learning styles.
Sometimes there is a tie-in with the university's academic specialties for on-site training.	If special facilities are needed, it will require shuttling people to an offsite location.
If conference center doesn't have sleeping rooms, you may need to look for nearby facilities and shuttle people.	Everything takes place under one roof—no need to shuttle people between facilities.
Sleeping facilities may be more stark with fewer amenities than same academics are used to, but costs are lower.	Sleeping rooms will be more luxurious; nicer amenities. Great to be pampered, but it has a price!

(continued)

Box 3.1 Continued

University Conference Center	*Outside Facility*
Typical meeting package costs $55-$60 per person/day, including room, food, snacks.	Typical room at hotel costs $100 per room per day, excluding food and beverages.
Facility may offer discounts to university faculty or affiliates.	Not many discounts.
Meeting planning arrangers at the facility may be inexperienced.	Facility planner is usually experienced.

SOURCE: Weiland (1993). Reprinted with permission from SUCCESSFUL MEETINGS Magazine. Copyright © 1993, Bill Communications, Inc.

When should you begin searching for a facility? As soon as you set the conference dates, especially if you will be meeting in a hotel. Many conference sites book 1, 2, 3, and even 10 years ahead.

Draw Up a Conference Prospectus to Give to the Facility

The first step in choosing a site is to draw up a *prospectus*, a summary about your meeting that is sent to the facilities before you arrive. Facility managers can serve you better when they know what you need, and they will know immediately if their properties will fit your meeting. When you arrive for the site inspection, they will be prepared and design tours to meet your needs. It will not take too long because many of the questions from both sides will already be answered.

Over the years, my prospectus for the conferences I plan has become a comprehensive guide with a series of questions. When I started planning meetings, a local board committee selected the site, usually with no contract. Sometimes it worked out fine, but many times the facility was a disaster. Nothing was written down, and we were at the mercy of the hotel. When the conference staff arrived to set up, we had many surprises. At one conference, the hotel staff had assigned the exhibits and a banquet to rooms that were directly over a train station. This led to some interesting times as a speaker tried to talk above the noise. In another conference, there was a choir rehearsal during workshop sessions, making it extremely difficult for the leaders and the attendees to hear. A prospectus was initiated after these experiences. Appendix C has a sample site prospectus that I use.

I include an extensive questionnaire in the prospectus that must be answered by the facility management and be appended to the contract. It covers the following areas and helps prevent misunderstandings: (a) contract, (b) meetings and exhibits, (c) freight storage, (d) catering/banquets/food outlets, (e) financial arrangements, and (f) sleeping rooms.

Next, include your program schedule with the prospectus. This gives the facility a feel for your meeting room needs.

The Site Visit

Why should you personally look at the facility sites? Each facility has unique characteristics, and you need to decide if it will fit your needs. Sometimes the facility dictates a change in your program. For example, if the hallways are narrow, it may be necessary to stagger breakout meeting times to avoid a bottleneck. If there is very little space for networking in the main lobby areas, you may need to plan additional receptions or mixers in a large ballroom.

Prepare a checklist of things to look for on your site visit. This will help you look for important things in the facility. If possible, try to visit the sites as close as you can to the time of the year you will be meeting so that you can get a feel for how your meeting would be conducted.

The list that follows covers major points to consider in choosing a facility. If you are interested in a more comprehensive checklist, please contact me through Sage (address on p. iv).

Checklist 3.2

Location and Appearance
- ☐ Distance of facility from transportation (airport, train station, parking lots), costs of transportation and/or parking
- ☐ Services available to guests

Meeting Rooms
- ☐ Access (stairs, elevators, escalators)
- ☐ Room capacities (maximum number of people in each room), types of setups
- ☐ Obstructions (pillars, etc.), staging area
- ☐ Location of light, temperature, and ventilation controls
- ☐ Exhibit space/setup (if used)
- ☐ Equipment and services available to the conference

Compliance With Americans With Disabilities Act and City Regulations
- ☐ Taxes, liquor laws, special licenses required, union requirements
- ☐ Setup for security and fire safety, access to fire escapes, location and number of sprinklers in rooms
- ☐ Evacuation plans in the event of a disaster
- ☐ Location of braille on elevators and doors
- ☐ Type of door openings: pull handles or doorknobs
- ☐ Bathroom facilities for physically challenged
- ☐ Facilities for the hearing impaired: blinking lights on phones and alarm clocks

Sleeping Rooms
- ☐ Number of single, double, triple, and quadruple rooms and suites
- ☐ Features for guest safety: peepholes in doors, deadbolt locks, doorframes flush against walls to avoid places for hiding
- ☐ Neatness of hallways (frequent pickup of room service trays)

Checklist 3.2 Continued

Local Services
☐ Public transportation
☐ Holidays (sometimes this can make a difference in numbers of restaurants that are open)

With your questions in hand, you are ready for the site inspections, walking through the facilities and meeting the facility representatives face-to-face. If possible, try to have two people on the site visit. It is an advantage because each person has a different perspective; also, with two people there is little chance that something will be overlooked. Before you go, try to learn some of the conference facility jargon. When you arrive at the facility, be prepared to take lots of notes. If you are looking at several sites, it will be necessary to write details about each facility. I have found it helpful to take either a video camera or a camera and a small tape recorder with me. The video camera has advantages because you can talk and film the site at the same time.

Another trick that is frequently used is to take the map of the facility when you are touring the site and to mark obstructions such as pillars, and so on. This is helpful when you need to make decisions on which program activity is best for each room. The tour then serves a double purpose for selecting a site and for planning the event should you decide to use the facility.

As you tour, remember one rule above all else:

Box 3.2

Put yourself in the place of your attendees. Look at the site through their eyes: the attendees, the physically challenged, the program leaders, and all who come to your event.

After you have toured the facilities, you need to consider other factors before you make your final site decision:

1. *Is the facility overbooked, or are there other competing meetings during the time you would be holding your conference?* This could be a disaster if you end up at the last minute with fewer meeting rooms than you had planned to use, or when you discover that many of your attendees cannot get sleeping rooms. Problems can also occur if there are two groups with conflicting agendas meeting simultaneously. I read about a facility that unwittingly put a National Day of Prayer group next to a room where the Adult Film Association was screening videos! Discuss any concerns you may have, and include a clause in the contract making the facility responsible to inform you of any competing meetings overlapping with yours.

2. *Ask about any plans for renovation or construction scheduled during the time you would meet.* The NCFR once had a meeting at a hotel that was in the middle of a major renovation that it did not know about when the meeting was scheduled. With jackhammers charging through cement, it was nearly impossible to hear the speakers.

3. *Be sure that the facility is in compliance with the American Disabilities Act (ADA).* The Department of Justice, which administers the ADA rules, considers meeting planners and committees partly responsible for fulfilling certain aspects of this act. Ask the facility to give you written details about their compliance with the ADA. Look at the guidelines of the ADA about your responsibilities at your conference.

4. *Check meeting room capacity charts for accuracy.* Sometimes, these charts greatly exaggerate the number of people that can fit into a meeting room. See Box 4.2 for general rules of thumb.

5. *Ask for a schedule of local events.* I read about one convention that had a drastic drop in attendance at the opening session. The reason was that many attendees were stuck on the other side of town when some city streets were closed for a local grand prix race.

6. *Check out political, labor, or management issues in the facilities.* Strikes, bankruptcies, racial disputes, or new ownership could ruin a meeting. If this happens, it is important that the members of the conference committee stay in close touch with each other and with the city convention and visitors bureau to prevent being caught in the middle or being blamed by both sides for a decision to proceed or abandon. One year, a conference had a city dispute occur about 10 months before its meeting was to take place. An ordinance was passed by the city council, banning nonresidents from using the city parks. The city residents were primarily White, and the ruling was interpreted as racist. A boycott ensued against all hotels and shopping malls in the city, and the organization was encouraged to move the conference from that site. However, it was impossible to find an alternative site at that late date. The law was challenged in the courts and was ruled unconstitutional about 2 weeks before the conference began. The organization stayed at the hotel, but many minority members used sleeping facilities elsewhere in protest.

7. *Check references.* Ask the facility for a list of other groups who have met there and call them. Get their honest opinions of how the facility and its management performed during their conference. Ask them how they felt about the facility's safety and security.

Get Everything You Negotiate in Writing

You are now ready to start narrowing down your search. Check through all your notes and photos or videos, decide on two to three key facilities, and ask them to send you a written contract. When you receive contracts from convention properties, *read them carefully from beginning to end.* Convention properties include university conference centers as well. Make a comparative chart of the properties on various sections of the contract.

The chart helps to see how properties are similar and different. See Appendix D for a sample. After comparing the contracts, you should narrow your choice to one site. In most cases it will be necessary to negotiate some features. No contract will ever be 100% to your liking. At my association, the contracts with the facilities are rewritten after their standard proposal has been received. One advantage is that all contracts are uniform; it forces you to *thoroughly read* the contract sent by the facility.

When you begin negotiating with the facility, write down the items you would like to see changed. Telephone the site and discuss the issues point by point. Eventually, you should come to a mutually satisfying agreement or pick another location.

Information to Be Included in a Contract

- Prices and rates for sleeping rooms, meeting room, and exhibit rental. Is meeting room rent on an hourly or a 24-hour basis?
- Labor charges for room setups, electricians, and so on.
- Mutual expectations of the conference and the facility regarding performance.
- Deadlines, including release dates for meeting room and sleeping room blocks.
- Mutual protection against unexpected events.
- Remedies for breach of contract or default on either side.
- Mechanisms to avoid future disputes.
- A cancellation clause. Properties build their budgets on anticipated income from convention contracts. If a convention cancels its meeting, properties may lose that income; therefore, they will insist on a cancellation clause. You may have to pay them some of their anticipated income if you do not use their facility and they cannot find another convention to take your place. Insist on a sliding scale so that up to 1 year before the convention meets you can cancel without financial penalty, with increasing penalties as the meeting date gets closer. The cancellation clause

should also state that, if the facility cancels the contract, they will make restitution to the organization and help them find an alternative site.

Tips for Contract Negotiations

- *Dates and days of the week.* Hotels operate according to the law of supply and demand. There are some peak seasons (highest occupancy), and sleeping rooms will be higher priced. Facilities will not be willing to make as many concessions if you must meet in their "prime time": generally September, October, November, April, and May. At those times there are many other events waiting in the wings, and facilities will not be as flexible. On the other hand, if you can hold your conference in the middle of the winter in the North, during the heat of the summer, or over a holiday period such as Thanksgiving, Christmas, or Easter, the facilities should be more flexible in rates because their business is generally slower.
- *The ratio of sleeping rooms to meeting room space needed.* If your conference requires all the meeting space of the facility, you will be expected to guarantee a minimum number of sleeping rooms or pay rental fees on meeting rooms. Over 70% of a hotel's gross income comes from sleeping room revenue. Do what you can to fill the sleeping rooms, or your rates will be higher.
- *The ratio of meeting rooms to catering functions.* A facility's next top revenue producer is catering. If you have few food functions, sleeping room prices will be higher, especially if your meeting takes all the facility's meeting space.
- *Discuss sleeping room rates first, then look at additional perks the facility will offer.* Before you begin negotiations with the facility, call the reservations department there and at other facilities around the area and ask about sleeping room prices. This rate is called the *rack rate* in facility jargon. Compare these rates with the rate that facilities are quoting for your conference. The conference or *group* rate should be considerably lower than the rack rate. Some facilities can offer in-kind concessions that can save you money and that are relatively inexpensive for them. Some standard concessions include one free sleeping room for

every 50 rooms used by your attendees, a free suite for the main speaker, discounted or free equipment rentals, and free labor for meeting room setups if the sleeping room block reaches a certain size. Another item you may be able to build into the contract might be handling gratuities yourself rather than building in service fees. Be realistic when you set aside a block of rooms for your group. Do not be too optimistic or pessimistic. This is where your records from previous conferences can help.

- *If the contract is for several years into the future, build in a ceiling on rates.* At today's prices, it can be advantageous to have a clause stating that rates will not increase above 5% per year for sleeping rooms, or 10% per year for food and beverage.
- *Be sure that those signing the contract have the authority to do so.* You may also wish to have a lawyer check over the contract before signing.
- *If you make changes in the original contract, be sure that both parties initial and date all changes.* It is a good idea then to rewrite the contract so that it is a clean copy. Make sure all changes are in writing.

Negotiations can be difficult, but when a contract is mutually satisfying to both parties, it is the beginning of a great partnership.

Transportation

For many of you who are planning a small meeting, your attendees may be driving to the facility. However, some of you may plan conferences where people will be flying in from many places. In this case, you may want to seek discounted airfares for attendees. Negotiating with the airlines or a travel agent may help save dollars for participants. They may also help your university or association pick up some perks like free plane tickets or a raffle prize. Most airlines also offer discounts for shipping your convention materials by air cargo if you sign a contract with them for discounted airfares.

You should also check on discounted rates for ground transportation to move people from the airport to the hotel, and/ or for rental cars.

Plan a Budget and Determine Expenses

After the site and the speakers have been selected, you can draw up a realistic budget. If the conference is to pay for itself, you need a budget to know how much to charge registrants. On the other hand, even if the conference is being funded by your college, you must know (a) the expenses to stay within the budget that has been allocated and (b) the true cost of the event.

The first step in budgeting is to determine the expenses you will have. Include the following:

- Speakers' fees (honoraria, travel, per diem)
- Meeting room rent
- Conference staff costs (salaries, benefits, travel)
- Publicity and marketing (typesetting, keylining, printing)
- Postage (mailing advance publicity, sending confirmation letters if necessary, shipping boxes to conference site)
- Food and beverage during the conference
- Insurance (unless covered under a blanket policy by your university)
- Awards
- Labor and gratuities for facility staff
- Supplies (computer, name badges, materials for packets, pencils, pens, staplers, staples, signs, etc.)
- Rental of audiovisual and other equipment
- Entertainment contracts, music licensing fees (if applicable), and other fees
- Rent, depreciation, and so on (if applicable)
- Miscellaneous expenses

Determine the Cost
of Registration for Participants

After the expenses have been checked, add the desired amount of profit if the conference is to realize a profit. The total is then divided by the expected number of attendees to develop a registration cost per person.

Once the registration fee is determined, it is possible that the registration cost per person is too high. At that time you will have to determine if there are ways to cut costs. This will be discussed in the next chapter.

Here are a few ways to cut the budget:

1. Schedule weekend conferences so that you can have the major speakers stay over a Saturday evening to cut airfares.
2. Negotiate complimentary sleeping rooms into the meeting facility contracts and use for staff and speakers.
3. Schedule meetings that require identical setups in the same room to cut labor costs.
4. Bring your own audiovisual equipment or rent it from the university or a local store rather than through the facility.

You can plan an economical conference that will be first-class. Planning a conference budget is similar to planning your own budget at home—trying to balance income and expenses.

After the site has been selected and the budget prepared, you are now ready to finalize the program schedule. The next chapter provides guidelines for planning a program that will benefit all attendees.

4 | Preparing the Program Schedule

Checklist 4.1

☐ Determine overall program structure; variety is the spice of life!
☐ Develop a grid of the program schedule.
☐ Preconference activities
☐ General sessions
☐ Breakout or discussion sessions
☐ Social activities and networking opportunities
☐ Ongoing sessions
☐ Committee meetings and miscellaneous activities
☐ Assign meeting rooms.
☐ Plan exhibits or book displays.
☐ Scrutinize the program; check for omissions and duplications.

In chapter 2, a brief discussion was given of planning a general program schedule so that you would know your needs before selecting a conference site. This chapter develops the planning process. There are guidelines for each of the steps.

Remember the one underlying rule in conference planning: *Always put yourself in the shoes of your attendees.*

Determine Overall Program Format

Some basic issues to think about as you begin to plan your program schedule are described below.

Program Content

- *Check the conference goals and secure speakers who can best fit those needs.* See the section on Selecting Speakers in chapter 2 for details on how to choose good speakers.
- *Remember that attendees want usable information.* Professionals want new ideas and the latest cutting edge information. The conference should have top-quality content and delivery.
- *Every meeting should include time for participants to voice their opinions in audience discussion.* Their feelings of commitment and empowerment lead to positive and constructive ideas. Keep audience interest by "mining the gold" from them.
- *Try to encourage a variety of speaker and presentation formats.* Attendees have a variety of learning styles. It is helpful to offer several types of formats.

Ways to Make the Schedule More Exciting

- *Have a stunning opening session, and a memorable, upbeat closing.* A well-planned, dynamic, informative opening session puts attendees in the mood to learn as much as they can during the conference. A challenging closing session will linger in attendees' memories as they focus on accomplishments and goals for the future. They will be ready to return to share new information with colleagues.
- *Keep sessions relatively short.* Two hours is usually the maximum that people can sit still. Attendees become tired and de-energized during long periods of listening.

- *Plan different formats to correspond with the body clock.* For instance, have interactive sessions immediately after lunch when attendees may be less attentive.
- *Try to schedule the program so that participants have good, but limited choices.* Give them real choices rather than conflicts. Try to have a balanced program that will appeal to the interests of as many attendees as possible. Do not schedule several sessions on one topic at the same time; spread them out over several time periods. When there are conflicts, attendees will be session hopping, which is very disturbing to speakers and other attendees. Those who go from one session to another will not get the full impact of any sessions they are attending. Check to see that program presenters are not scheduled to be in two places at once.
- *Allow a minimum of 15 to 20 minutes between sessions so that attendees can easily get from one meeting to another.* Thirty minutes is more desirable. People do not appreciate being late for sessions, but if the schedule is too tight, it is almost impossible to arrive on time.
- *Plan free time for networking.* Some of the best conference experiences come from interchange with others. If possible, leave mealtimes free so that people can have time to get together. Another way to encourage networking is to have planned refreshment breaks.
- *Consider having evening sessions to help alleviate the scheduling crunch.*

Develop a Grid of the Program Schedule

You are now ready to begin the task of putting together the schedule. I will explain the manual process, although there are software packages available for scheduling and facility management. Contact the American Society of Association Executives (ASAE) for a list of consultants in its *Buyer's Guide.* ASAE's address is listed in Appendix J.

Begin with a grid of the entire program schedule by time slots and days (Box 4.1). Set up the grid so that you can see the whole picture. Pencil in everything; the schedule usually changes many times.

You are now ready to begin planning your program.

Preconference Activities

Preconference activities serve many purposes. A hospitality room, set up before the conference begins, can be used as a gathering place for attendees who arrive early. This is a great place to become acquainted with new people and find out about their work. Some people like to have time to go sightseeing. It is nice to be able to go into the hospitality room, talk to someone who knows where good restaurants are located, and pick up brochures about local sites.

A good preconference activity is an in-depth half-day or full-day workshop or training session. Usually, sessions during the conference are shorter and give more of an overview. The preconference workshop, on the other hand, can give both theoretical and practical applications on a focused topic.

Committee meetings can be held prior to the conference.

Get-acquainted no-host receptions can be planned as icebreakers for the early birds.

General Sessions

It is important to intersperse general sessions and breakouts throughout the day. Be thoughtful of your attendees. It is physically impossible to retain knowledge if the same activity is carried out for several hours without a change.

General or *main sessions* have all attendees present in one session. Nothing else is scheduled during those times.

You may have one expert or a panel of three or four individuals present a specific topic. In a panel, each participant discusses one area of a broader topic, and a moderator summarizes and links the talks. The topics of your speakers fit your conference theme.

Allow time in these sessions for questions and audience discussion. The time for the speaker(s) should be limited to 50 to 60 minutes.

Box 4.1

1994 NCFR Program Schedule
Friday, November 11

7 am	8 am	9 am	10 am	11 am	12 pm	1 pm	2 pm	3 pm	4 pm	5 pm	6 pm	7 pm	8 pm	9 pm
30 45	00 15 30 45	00 15 30 45	00 15 30 45	00 15 30 45	00 15 30 45	00 15 30 45	00 15 30 45	00 15 30 45	00 15 30 45	00 15 30 45	00 15 30 45	00 15 30 45	00 15 30 45	00 15 30 45
Focus Groups III					Focus Groups IV					Focus Groups V				
Committee Meetings														
			Plenary Session and Discussion Time		Visit the Exhibits		**Special Panel - Indian Family Life**							
	Papers IV				Papers V				Papers VI					
	Symposia IV					Teaching Round Tables			Symposia V					
					Posters II									
										Section Membership Meetings III				
					S/NP Seminar				S/NP Development Forum					
					Association of Councils Workshop									
										Special Sessions				

Usually, it is best to schedule main sessions at a reasonable hour in the morning (between 9:00 a.m. and 10:30 a.m.). This is especially important when the topics are research oriented or technical in nature. Most people tend to be more attentive and able to better retain information after a night's rest. One word of caution: Do not schedule important speakers too early, even though the best learning is in the morning. Few attendees arrive on time or are very attentive if you schedule main speakers before 9:00 a.m.

There are good, fresh alternative formats for main sessions, which can maximize the impact of the main speaker or panel.

- *Max-mix seating* promotes interaction and involvement. The room is set in round tables rather than theater style. The speaker or the panelists are at the front of the room. Attendees sit at the round tables. The first part of the session is devoted to the speaker or the panelists. The second part focuses on 10-minute group discussions at each round table led by facilitators who have prepared discussion questions. Each facilitator summarizes the discussion at his or her table. Everyone then returns together for a summary of the small group discussion.

- *Round table forum* involves a panel of speakers seated in a circle in the center of the room. The audience is seated in an outer circle. During the first part of the session, the panel members talk among themselves about a topic, and the audience listens and takes notes. A facilitator asks the panelists specific questions during this time. At a specified time period, the audience asks questions of the panelists.

- *Audience reaction team* has 4 or 5 participants quiz the main speaker from the stage with some typical audience questions.

- *Colloquium* has two groups of 3 to 4 individuals interacting. One side represents the audience, and the other is the panel of experts.

- *Debate* has panelists divide into two groups: One represents the pro side of an issue, the other represents the con.

- *Interview* has a moderator, on behalf of the audience, who questions the speaker. (Adapted from Simmons, 1989b)[1]

I have suggested these ideas to make your sessions interesting. If you want to try anything new, be sure that you ask the speakers if they are willing and able to adapt to the new format.

Breakout Sessions

These are smaller sessions that are led by one or more persons; they are designed to provide audience interaction. Breakouts fulfill an important part of adult learning. Participants feel more comfortable in a small group of their peers and may be more willing to share their own thoughts. There are usually several concurrent breakouts, enabling attendees to attend sessions in which they have specific interests. Try to provide at least 50% of the conference scheduling to allow for choices.

Breakouts should allow for as much guided audience participation as possible. They can be a place where practical applications for new research can be presented. At most breakout sessions, presenters are requested to provide handouts that summarize the research and give practical implications.

There are several ways to make breakouts more meaningful for attendees: Be sure the presenters draw implications, discuss new options, and develop applications. You can also assign someone to be a session recorder. He or she will take notes during the session and write a summary to be produced in *Conference Proceedings* or in interorganization newsletters.

Using a variety of formats and techniques can be more satisfying to your attendees. Some alternative breakout sessions to the traditional lecture or panel include the following:

- *Symposia:* These are presentations by 3 to 4 individuals, organized by a chair who leads the discussion. The presenters each discuss a different facet of the topic, and a discussant integrates the papers to each other and the topic.

- *Role-play:* Participants act out a real-life situation in front of the audience. The audience discusses the implications to the problem being portrayed.

- *Listening team:* Individuals are selected before the session to listen and to take notes during the presentations and then question or summarize after the speeches.

- *Posters:* These are reports of work summarized in graphic form. Attendees move about the posters and discuss the projects with the authors on a one-to-one basis.

- *Resource exchange:* This is a specialized poster presentation for introducing program designs, curricula and materials, teaching techniques, and evaluation methods and outcomes.

- *Round tables:* These are informal sessions with 1 or 2 presenters and 8 to 10 attendees who are seated at a table. The presenters give an overview of a topic and then lead the group into a discussion. You can vary this by having participants switch tables during the course of the session.

Social Activities and Networking Opportunities

One of the benefits of attending a conference is networking. In academia, it is especially important to make contacts with others in your field. Conferences must contain some social activities, or attendees will skip sessions to network. Receptions and mixers provide a sense of unity and reenergize the group. A little relaxation helps to clear the mind.

Selecting the right social events is challenging—especially if there is a limited budget. Try to schedule at least one social event at the beginning of the conference to help people get acquainted.

A few rather inexpensive options include the following:

- *An activity for first-time attendees* to allow them to meet program participants, longtime members, and other people like themselves who have never been to your conference before.

- *Receptions* give people opportunities to visit. It is nice to have hosts who go around the room looking for attendees who seem to be by themselves, initiate conversations, and introduce them to others.

- A *theme party* lends a nice touch to the conference. Check with the meeting facility for suggestions that are typical of the locale. They often have props left over from other conferences that can be used for your event. Announce the event in advance.
- For a small university conference you may wish to have a *talent (or untalent) show* where attendees provide the entertainment. It is interesting to see the variety of talent. An emcee makes introductions and plans the program so that acts will tie together.

These are just a few suggestions. Chapter 7 discusses how to book entertainment.

Ongoing Events

When you plan the schedule, remember to schedule times and rooms for the services that run continuously throughout the conference such as job service, press room, hospitality room, and so on. If your program is full, you may wish to extend the hours for these services so that more attendees can use them.

The job service is particularly popular at most meetings. Chapter 1 described how attendees can best use it. At the NCFR, the employment service begins during the preconference and runs 12 hours a day throughout the conference. This service could generate revenue if you charged a fee.

Committee Meetings
and Miscellaneous Activities

Try to plan these events when you do not have other conference sessions. Attempt to accommodate requests from other groups, but you must make your own sessions top priority. Late evening or early morning hours can be ideal times for these meetings and events.

Most facilities prefer to have only one person (or committee) making arrangements with them for the entire conference. When you plan meetings and/or receptions of smaller or related groups, send order sheets to those chairing the events. Ask them to give your committee the orders for food; preferred times for meeting; and the names, addresses, and phone numbers of those planning the function. The order sheets are then returned to you. Incorporate their orders into your staging guide (see chapter 6, "Last-Minute Advance Preparations").

Assign Meeting Rooms

Once the program is planned, it is necessary to assign sessions to specific rooms. I set up another grid by room, time, and date (see Appendix E). Think about the guidelines as you assign rooms, and pencil everything on the grid. Even though there are some software programs available, many meeting planners prefer doing it manually to plan the best use of rooms for the individual situation.

It is important to carefully plan the layouts for each session. When attendees enter a meeting room, they immediately have a feel for what will be happening in the session. Try to assign the proper size room for each event, although there are times when this is not possible. Consider the following when you try to match meeting rooms to your sessions:

- *Dimensions of the room and the square footage.* Use the rules of thumb listed in the next section to determine the capacities of rooms. Do not use figures from the facility maps for this. Their figures are based on a maximum capacity established by the city fire marshall.
- *Windows, barriers, and decor of the room can determine the type of function.* Rooms without barriers are flexible for any type of function. If there are pillars or other barriers in the room, you should use these for receptions, exhibits, and so on where the audience does not need to see a speaker. Elaborate rooms with mirrors, chandeliers, gaudy furnishings, carpet, and wall and window

treatments may be nice for banquets, but they are distracting for breakout sessions. If you are having a reception or banquet with speakers at a head table, you need a barrier-free room so that everyone can see the speaker. Rooms with a wall of windows should not be used for sessions using audiovisual equipment. If a large room breaks down into four or five smaller ones, you need to check out the soundproofing of the air walls between the sections. It is annoying to have a soft-spoken speaker in one section and a rock band in the adjacent room. If you have one of several meetings in the facility, ask about the program planned for the rooms next to yours so that you can avoid disaster.

- *Facilities for the physically challenged.* All properties are required by law to be accessible for handicapped persons, but some are easier to access than others. If you know there will be several attendees using wheelchairs, use rooms that could easily accommodate them.
- *Traffic flow between rooms.* If there are narrow hallways and you have several concurrent sessions, you may need to stagger the sessions to avoid bottlenecks.
- *Rest room accessibility.*
- *Convenience of food and beverage services.*

The following figures should be taken into account when calculating room capacity:

Box 4.2

Calculating Room Capacity

- Allow 10 square feet per person for theater-style seating. With theater-style seating, chairs only are set up in rows facing the head table or stage. More people can fit in a room with this type of seating.
- Allow 40 to 45 square feet per person for conference-style seating. In this setup, tables are set in a rectangle or oval shape with chairs on both sides and ends.

(continued)

Box 4.2 Continued

- Allow 22 to 25 square feet per person for schoolroom style. This is a common setup for all-day seminars. Tables are lined up in a row, one behind the other on each side of a center aisle with chairs facing the head table.
- Allow 12 to 15 square feet per person if the room will be set up with round tables. Round tables are used for banquets or discussion sessions.

These figures allow for a raised platform, a speakers' table, and simple audiovisual equipment such as an overhead or slide projector and a screen. More space is needed when elaborate equipment is used, for example, for rear screen projection. There are several convention planning books that give specific formulas for setting up rooms. I use *The CLC Manual* (1989, 5th ed.), published by the Convention Liaison Council, as a reference. Meeting Planners International (MPI) has a handy guide for figuring room capacities. See Appendixes J and K for the addresses of CLC and MPI.

After you have assigned the rooms, send the schedule to the convention service manager at the conference facility. He or she will be able to tell you if everything can be worked out with efficiency. Ask for help with room setups. Facility staff have prepared for many conferences and may have ideas that you have not even considered.

Plan Exhibits or Displays

The publishing industry plays an important role in the academic world. One of the requirements for advancement is to have articles and books published. To grow professionally, it is necessary to read the latest material and use it in the classroom. You may wish to have a book exhibit at your confer-

---

Box 4.3

"The key to a successful exhibit is to bring together the right buyers and the right sellers."

—Simmons (1989a)[2]

---

ence, so that your attendees can be exposed to new materials. Attendees hear about new books during the sessions, and if they see them during your conference, they may buy them immediately.

Publishers consider exhibiting at an academic conference a great market for selling their products, because it is often the only occasion when their customers can browse through the actual books rather than examine descriptions in a catalog. Many attendees may be well-known writers whose books can be featured by their publishers. In addition to being a place where attendees eagerly review new materials, your conference gives publishers the opportunity to interview potential authors.

If you have time in your program, and space in your meeting facility, you may wish to consider including exhibits. Exhibitors are partners at the conference.

You do not need an elaborate setup to offer a book exhibit. You may wish to begin by simply offering a tabletop exhibit where individual book titles are displayed and order blanks are provided. You may also wish to show new videos along with the book exhibit. More complicated exhibits with full-draped booths are more expensive, but exhibitor fees can be a source of revenue for the conference. One option at a small conference is to ask your campus or local bookstore to set up the display.

You will need to build exhibit costs into your overall conference budget if you offer this service for your attendees. Consider the following as you plan an exhibit:

1. Find out what your attendees are interested in buying, and contact suppliers who can provide what you need. Bringing in products that are unrelated to your conference is a costly waste of exhibitors' time and money.

2. When you contact prospective publishers and suppliers, give them an accurate profile of your attendees. A few years ago, some publishers exhibited at many conferences, often to show their support, but today's economy has changed that picture. Exhibiting at a conference is costly. The companies must pay the exhibitor's fee; ship the display and products; and cover additional fees for decorating, furniture, and storage of the materials. They also must pay the transportation, the sleeping accommodations, and the meals of their representatives. To justify attending, suppliers must be able to show a solid return on their investment.

3. Prepare attractive publicity material. Your brochures should tell prospective exhibitors what they can expect from your attendees. Describe the advantages of exhibiting at your conference. Give them information about your conference. Describe the conference location, dates, persons responsible for the exhibit, your requirements, details about exhibit space, and a reservation form. If you are selling full exhibit booths, send a contract and an exhibitor manual at least 3 months ahead of time. Include order forms for service; shipping instructions; times for setting up and tearing down the exhibit; fire regulations; insurance and liability requirements; and availability of contractors for furniture, carpeting, cleaning, and receptions.

4. On receiving reservations from exhibitors (either full exhibit, or publishers sending copies of a few book titles), acknowledge receiving the reservation and maintain contact with them.

5. If you are using a pipe-and-drape display (a booth with a backdrop of fabric) for your exhibit, secure an official service contractor. Check local laws to be sure you are in compliance with their ordinances. The contractor provides "pipe and drape" and an attractive entrance to the exhibit room, sets up

the room, prepares a layout of the exhibit area in compliance with local fire regulations, and gives assistance to the exhibitors as they set up and tear down their booths. Ask the hotel or facility for their recommendation on who to use.

6. Ask one or two people to be on-site coordinators to give exhibitors assistance and to answer attendees' questions.

7. Work cooperatively with exhibitors to encourage attendees to visit the exhibits by scheduling free time. A high volume of traffic is the key to success for exhibitors.

- Try to put the exhibits in a high-traffic area in the midst of conference activities.
- Set aside times in the program where the only event is visiting the exhibits.
- Have drawings for prizes in the exhibit area with prizes possibly donated by the exhibitors.
- Turn the exhibit area into an informal meeting area available for participants with beverages and light food.
- Set poster sessions adjacent to the exhibits so that the traffic can flow from one into the other.

Do all you can to make your exhibitors feel welcome.

8. Give free registration to all exhibitors. Involve them in all the sessions, including asking publishers to organize a session on "Tips for Publishing."

9. Ask exhibitors for their evaluation of both the exhibits and the conference.

Scrutinize the Program; Recheck for Omissions and Duplications

After everything has been scheduled, I check the program again and review the following steps in scheduling:

1. Review the conference goals and choose the main speakers. Plan dynamic opening and closing sessions.

2. Select the breakout sessions from abstracts that have been submitted. Try to have a variety of formats throughout the program to appeal to all the attendees.

3. Set up a program grid to plan the sessions. Keep sessions to a maximum of 2 hours. Build the schedule in the following order:

- Preconference activities.
- General sessions in the morning.
- Concurrent sessions with a variety of topics. Do not overlap topics. Be sure that speakers are not scheduled to present two papers at the same time. Alternate formats. Do not plan consecutive lecture sessions. Have interactive sessions immediately after lunch.
- Breaks, social activities, and networking opportunities.
- Ongoing events.
- Committee meetings and miscellaneous activities.

After you have finished, look at the balance. Are there too many lecture sessions together? Is there enough time for people to get to sessions? Are there too many sessions on one subject? Are some of the speakers scheduled at the same time? Keep reviewing and changing the program until it looks appealing.

4. Assign meeting rooms for each of the sessions, using a room/time chart. Think about size and type of room and match it to the program. Be sure to include networking sessions, ongoing activities, and exhibits in your plan. After you have finished, carefully review the chart. Think about the following:

- Are there any rooms where two sessions are scheduled simultaneously?
- Do you have sessions scheduled in the same rooms with identical formats?
- Is there enough time for the facility staff to change the room setups? For example, if you have a session set theater style from

10:00 a.m. to 12:00 p.m., do not schedule a luncheon in that room beginning at 12:15 p.m.; it takes a minimum of 1 to 2 hours for the staff to change to a banquet.

A well-planned program is the key to a successful conference. If you try to be creative in scheduling, you will have a dynamic program that will attract registrants. The next chapter will discuss how to market your special event.

Notes

1. Adapted with permission of the Convention Liaison Council (CLC) from *The CLC Manual*. The complete manual is available from the CLC, 1575 Eye St. NW, Washington, DC 20005. Send $22.95 with your order.

2. Reprinted with permission of the Convention Liaison Council (CLC) from *The CLC Manual*. The complete manual is available from the CLC, 1575 Eye St. NW, Washington, DC 20005. Send $22.95 with your order.

5 | Promotion and Marketing

Checklist 5.1

☐ Build a marketing plan with schedule based on conference goals, attendees, format, and content.
☐ Create promotional materials and ads.
☐ Implement marketing plan.
☐ Plan publicity.
☐ Implement publicity.
☐ Track response and follow-up.

The best planned program will be a dismal failure if no one attends. This chapter briefly highlights important elements of marketing your meeting. If you are hosting a small conference with invited participants, you may not need to go through all these steps of promotion, but you still want to send attractive printed materials in advance to the attendees. Most conferences, however, need to publicize their events to attract registrants. Adapt these principles to your specific needs.

A colleague in the meetings industry once told me that the main purpose of a promotional piece is to make it so attractive that it gets beyond the trash can. Her point was that there is such a proliferation of unsolicited mail that most people do not have time to read everything. Unless a mailing piece catches the reader's eye as being something worthy of being opened and read, the general response is to throw it out—unopened.

Build a Marketing Plan With Schedule

Generally 5% to 10% of a conference budget should be spent on marketing. It is important to carefully plan how you will spend these precious dollars. The best way is to develop an overall marketing plan that discusses *the ways* you will tell about your conference to attract attendees. A marketing plan is similar to human relationships: You must have an approach and good timing.

Include the following information as you prepare your plan:

- *Background material.* Include all the basic information discussed in chapter 2 on purpose, goals, objectives of the conference, your audience, and the program.
- *Opportunities.* You will want to compare your conference with others being held. What unique ideas, activities, or benefits does your program offer that others do not? What will participants get out of your conference?
- *Marketing strategy.* Include the creative strategy and marketing tools to reach your goal.
- *Implementation plan.* Write down how your program will be carried out. Use the five W's: *Who, What, When, Where, Why.* (Mitchell, 1985)

Define Your Audience

When you defined your conference goals, you thought about the people who would benefit the most from your conference (your audience). In your marketing plan the most important element is making sure your publicity reaches the *right* audience. Your promotional materials should include information to make people want to come to the event, but they must also be worded in a way to show the value of the conference so that department heads and deans will grant permission to attend. As you prepare promotional materials, make them appeal to the needs of your audience.

Direct Mail

As you prepare a marketing plan, you need to look for the right approaches to reach this audience. For most academic conferences, direct mail can be a valuable communication medium. Most people remember more of what they see than what they hear. A written mailer has tangible information that can be filed or reread. It is easy to track direct mail marketing. Mailers can be coded, and you can test new lists, designs of the brochures, and changes in timing the mailings to measure their effectiveness.

Analyze the attendees from past conferences if you have had them. Many planners have discovered that 80% of those who attend their conferences come from within a 300-mile radius. This is not surprising with today's economy and the shrinking or nonexistent academic funding for conferences. If you have access to other attendee information such as job title or professional affiliations, you can look for the best persons to contact for your coming event.

The lists most likely to yield results are of (a) people who attended the previous conference, if there was one, or similar conferences you have planned before; (b) members of professional associations in your field; and (c) those who share the demographics of the attendees who attended the last similar conference sponsored by your department or university. Marketing also depends on the type of conference you are sponsoring. You may be able to exchange mailing lists with other universities or professional associations. If your budget includes adequate funding, you may wish to rent lists from direct mail brokers, professional associations, and other universities who charge for their mailing lists. Usually, these lists can be selected by the demographic variables you choose.

You must remember that you will have to mail to a large list to gain your anticipated number of registrants. Marketing experts differ in theories of responses. Some say mail information to 10 times the number of people who want to attend the conference. Others say a good mailing list response is 2%. Others say that you must make seven contacts to equal one registration.

Creating Brochures

There are tricks of the trade that help a brochure look professional and clean. If your university has a journalism school, a public relations office, and/or a graphic arts department, ask if they will help you write and prepare your materials. You can also employ the services of a small quick printer.

It is helpful to file interesting flyers and ads from other conferences, to use as examples when designing your own material.

When preparing direct mail pieces, be sure they discuss two things: (a) benefits of attending and (b) how to register. Tell people what to do, when to do it, and how it should be done. Conference brochures create an impression about the meeting and your university or association. If the piece is crammed with information and confusing, people will not take the time to read it. The brochure has one goal: to generate attendance at your meeting. Keep the design as simple as possible, and make the copy come alive; the flyer should be enthusiastic, upbeat, and dynamic. Use short, punchy sentences. Be brief. Use pictures and graphics to make a point, not just to fill up space.

Use two contrasting typefaces, bold type, bullets, screening, and boxes to draw attention to important points at a glance. Try to vary the layout so that it is interesting, and leave some white space.

If you are able to send the piece by bulk mail, be sure to have the bulk mailing indicia and proper wording included in your brochure. Check with your university or local post office for details on proper mailing procedures. Remember that bulk mail takes longer to be delivered than first-class mail: Adjust your schedule accordingly.

Developing the Message

The cover should be simple and forthright with information about the theme and the topic, the date, the time, the place, and the sponsor of the conference. You may wish to put a short invitation at the bottom of the cover, for example, "Don't miss this important conference."

Include a concise statement about the purpose of the conference and perhaps some short background information about your university or association's reputation to sponsor it.

List the personal benefits of attendance. Do not make a dry list of features. Use action verbs as in a résumé format such as "share," "learn," "participate," and so on.

Outline the program highlights.

Include information about the conference facility and the surrounding campus, the city, and the area. If attendees will need to stay overnight, give the telephone number for making reservations, or include housing reservation forms or flyers about nearby facilities.

Short testimonials from people who have attended previous conferences you have sponsored can be effective when they sell the event, for example, "I learned," or "I was able to bring this to my staff."

Include a conference registration form (with a deadline date) in the mailing piece.

It is wise to frequently repeat the conference dates, the place, the theme, and the sponsor throughout the brochure. Be sure to list several times in the brochure a phone and fax number as well as the address where people can obtain additional information. If you have early bird registration/late fees, include this in your mailing piece.

Registration Form

Make it simple by using checkoff boxes arranged in columns rather than filling in the blank spaces. You may wish to place codes on the form to identify which lists attracted registrants.

Highlight key information on the form. Try to keep as much white space as possible for ease in completion.

Include the following information:

1. Name, date, and location of event.
2. Space for registrant to fill in biographical information: name, address, zip or postal code, employer, phone number, and other items you need to have for the conference.
3. Costs for each type of registration, special events, and any additional fees such as continuing education credits. Be sure costs are immediately visible.
4. Registration deadline and additional fees charged after the cutoff date.
5. Cancellation and refund policy.
6. Place for entering total amount due and method of payment: checks, cash, credit card number and expiration date, phone and fax number (if you allow registrations by these methods with a credit card).
7. Address where registrations should be returned and clear, concise instructions for filling out the registration form.

Tracking Results

Once the mailings have been sent, monitor the results. You should begin receiving registrations in approximately 2 to 5 weeks. If you were able to place codes on the brochure and registration form, write down the responses as they come in so you can evaluate the effectiveness of each mailing list you used. Begin making follow-up phone calls to some key people on your list, or send them a personalized letter and call them later. Today's technology makes it easy to individualize letters through word processing mail merge. Record the responses.

Other Methods

News Releases and Press Conferences

An initial press release should be sent to universities and professional associations and should include essentials of the meeting and the who, what, when, where, why; date, time, place, theme, major speakers, and address and phone number to contact for more information.

Reaching the media can be difficult for an academic conference planner. Editors are looking for a shell from a news release that can be developed into a story quickly. The five W's (who, what, when, where, and why) should be answered in the first paragraph. The lead sentence tells the editor why this story would interest his or her audience. Develop a conference *fact sheet* in outline format to include with the press release. Ask your university public relations department to help you write these pieces.

Press conferences can help the university and your conference, or they can be a disaster. It is best to call a news conference only if you are releasing truly interesting or *new* findings that will benefit the public, or if there is important information on a hot topic that is mentioned almost daily. Make sure the presentation is short and open for questions. No one should have to read a paper. The information *must* be a digest. Otherwise it is best not to have one.

Ads

Advertising in other publications can be an effective way to let others know about your conference, because ads reach a large number of readers. Because of the high cost of ads, it is important to carefully plan the publications that will reach the best audience for your conference. The NCFR places its ads in its own journals and newsletters and seeks to exchange advertising in the publications of organizations who share similar goals. The NCFR also purchases ads in journals with a readership that has an interest in the NCFR's theme for the year. This strategy could be used for academic conferences. Advertising copy for publication must include the basic who, what, when, where, and why. Follow the same guidelines as for brochures, but remember that space is limited. All information must be consolidated. It is wise to have someone with design experience help you create ads.

Telemarketing, Radio, Public Events

There are other means of marketing your conference, but you must be careful to determine if they are right for your conference. If you are trying to reach only professors of universities, then the use of magazines, radio, television, and so on may be ineffective. I will briefly describe some of these publicity strategies, and you can adapt your marketing plan to your situation.

Work closely with the publicity department of the university to determine which of these publicity strategies to use.

One of the best times to promote your conference is at another university-sponsored event. You can prepare a flyer to insert in registration packets, or you can leave flyers on a table with giveaways for others to pick up. Capitalize on the conference enthusiasm to announce your upcoming event.

A relatively new way to market conferences is through the use of telemarketing. This can be effective if you follow a few rules: (a) Those making the calls should be fully informed about all aspects of your conference so that they can answer questions intelligently and quickly. They need to have good telephone skills and think well on their feet. (b) Develop an accurate, targeted file of phone numbers to most effectively reach the right people. Telemarketing is a way to gauge the interest and quality of leads. You can determine from the phone conversation if people are interested in attending; send the mailing piece to the ones who are.

Magazine advertising creates an image or communicates an idea. When you promote a conference you want registrations—action! This can be difficult to achieve from ads. An exception to this rule is advertising in your own publications because you can hit the same audience several times at little cost.

Newspaper ads are effective if you want to reach the public; however, generally, they are an expensive, less effective way to publicize a small academic conference. Television and radio advertising can be very expensive and not as effective for promotion of a specialized event unless your campus owns its own station.

Set Up Your Promotion Schedule, Based on the Marketing Plan

It is best if you have a minimum of 4 to 6 months to promote a conference. One year is optimum. You can then send a series of mailings to your prospect list so that people are frequently reminded of your event.

Here is a tentative calendar based on a 6-month plan. If you have less time, it will be necessary to combine several steps.

6 months before the conference
1. Send first news release to universities and professional associations.
2. Send major mailing piece to your entire prospect list.
3. Send exhibit brochure to prospective exhibitors.

4 months before the conference
1. Send second news release to universities and professional associations.

2. Create a cover story about the conference in your own publication, promoting the benefits of attendance.

3 months before the conference

1. Place advertisements in university and professional association publications. The *Chronicle of Higher Education* is a good resource for academic events.
2. Make follow-up phone calls to prospective exhibitors and advertisers.

2½ months before the conference

1. Identify key media people in the local area. Call first to determine if they are interested in publicizing your conference.

2 months before the conference

1. Send invitations to key media list. Offer complimentary registration and admission to all functions. Outline the conference. Highlight any sessions that deal with local or regional issues.
2. Send follow-up mailing to people on your prospect list within a 300-mile radius.

3 weeks before the conference

1. Send follow-up news release to the media. Highlight sections of the program that are of interest to their reporters.

2 weeks before the conference

1. Follow-up phone calls to key media.

During the conference

1. Set up a media center. Keep in touch with the media. Invite them to attend.

Publicity is a key element in the success of a conference. Building and implementing your marketing plan is the first of the steps in advance conference preparations. After the publicity and the registration forms have been mailed, you are ready to begin processing registrations. The next chapter will outline this process and other preparations before the conference.

6 | Last-Minute Advance Preparations

Checklist 6.1

☐ Avoid undue stress by preparing as much as possible before you leave for the conference.
☐ Process advance registrations.
☐ Secure child-care options for attendees who request it.
☐ Plan food functions. Prepare function sheets for the facility.
☐ Prepare staging guide of meeting room setups to send to facility manager.
☐ Prepare directional signs, printed programs, materials for packets, rosters of attendees (if used).
☐ Prepare registration packets and print name badges.
☐ Prepare assignments for conference staff and conduct first staff meeting.
☐ Write out announcements and other instructions for session presiders.
☐ Make arrangements to pick up keynote speakers.

Once the program is planned and the event promoted and publicized, it is important to begin working on logistical details immediately. The better prepared you are in advance, the more smoothly the conference will run. This chapter provides guidelines on how to handle the basic last-minute tasks that need to be done. The timetable is based on the assumption that you have at least 2 to 3 months to prepare for the conference. You will need to adjust your time line accordingly. If your conference is for 30 to 40 people, it will not take as much time to do some of the tasks as one with 1,000 attendees, but the basic steps are the same. Try to work as far ahead as possible to avoid the last-minute rush. Many things cannot be done until just before the conference: Do what you can early!

Eight to Twelve Weeks
Before the Conference

Process Registrations
and Plan for On-Site Registration

In chapter 5, the design of the registration form was discussed. Before the forms are printed, you must have the registration process in place. Decide whether you will handle registrations manually or by computer. The registration system should be able to perform the following tasks:

- Monitor finances, generate receipts, and have forms for reconciling cash. Produce an accurate financial report on the conference.
- Update numbers and types of registrations.
- Generate alphabetic registration lists. List and monitor attendance at conference sessions and special events for which attendees sign up.
- Generate name badges and tickets for special events, confirmation letters, and invoices.
- Generate reports and mailing labels needed for all facets of the conference.

There are many meeting management software packages available. Check with the ASAE for a list of consultants in their Buyer's Guide. The ASAE's address is listed in Appendix J. If you purchase software, remember that the computer should work for you, not vice versa.

Your system for processing registrations should be similar for both preregistrations and on-site registrations.

When you begin receiving registration forms and payment, record the date received. If you have special events with limited space, monitor this carefully. Usually, these are filled on a first-come, first-serve basis. Be sure to bring original registration forms with you to the conference, even if you are using a computerized system. These forms are a backup when questions arise.

Try to process registrations regularly so that there will not be a last-minute rush just prior to the conference. It also helps to avoid errors.

Secure Child-Care Options
for Attendees Who Require This Service

In some conferences, attendees may bring their small children and need child care while they are in meetings. There are several alternatives:

- Arrange for an outside service located near the conference facility.
- Have child-care providers come to the facility to take care of the children.
- Hire students from a local college/university child development department or a civic group willing to care for children.

When checking into child-care options, ask about the following: (a) references, (b) costs, (c) hours, (d) insurance coverage by the child-care provider and type of waiver to be signed by parents (Providers must have adequate insurance so that the conference sponsor and facility are held harmless against liability), (e) compliance with state child-care laws.

Prepare Directional Signs

Good signage helps attendees find their way and know what to do. When attendees are confused about where to go they become frustrated. Always put yourself in the attendees' shoes when you are trying to decide what signs to make.

Start from the entrance and work your way through the entire facility. Be sure that signs include instructions on where to go and what to do. Use arrows and color codes if the facility is confusing or has many levels for meeting rooms. It is a good idea to print the name of your conference, and logo if you have one, at the top of each sign.

Attendees enjoy having signs beside each room entrance that list a daily schedule of events. Use a clear plastic sheet protector for each room. File the event lists in date order in each protector. At the end of each day, remove the sign from the sleeve so that the current day's list is on top.

Signs can be very expensive. For the conferences I plan, generally professionally lettered signs are made for those that are reused, such as registration instructions and identification signs for ongoing events and services. It is nice to have a large banner announcing the conference that can be set up in an area where attendees can easily see it. If your conference has a generic name, it will pay to purchase one that will last for several years. There are many companies who specialize in banners, and prices will vary greatly. If your conference is for one time only, attractive banners can be made inexpensively from felt or paper or on computer. Check with the art department at your university about making your signs or banners. They may be happy to do these as projects with their students.

Location and directional signs can be done on the computer and laser printer. Print them in the largest type possible to fit on the standard sheet and take it to a local quick-print shop for enlargement. This is an inexpensive process, but the signs look professional. With today's computer and printer technology, it is rarely necessary to have these professionally prepared.

Plan the Food Functions

Food and beverage functions are more than just food or beverages; they are events that provide the primary mechanism for networking at a conference. Attendees meet new associates and renew acquaintances, exchange ideas, and discover solutions to problems. If these functions are a hit, the attendees will have positive feelings toward the conference. You and your committee are the official hosts of the events. Your challenge is to provide attractive settings, imaginative menus, and an atmosphere conducive to socializing. Most facilities are unwilling to quote firm menu prices more than 3 months ahead of time because of varying food costs, but they will give you estimates at any time. It is important to remember that in most hotels or conference centers, it is a requirement that you must use only their food. You cannot bring in food from the outside. If they make an exception and allow you to bring it in, they may bill a corkage fee (a fee they charge to bring the cost up to their prices).

Several factors influence the cost of food and beverages for food functions and the restaurants and room service in the facility: (a) location of the facility (those in large cities may be able to obtain better prices for food, but the market can be more expensive); (b) the season (for example, do not expect strawberry shortcake to be the same price in January as it is in June); (c) size of facility; (d) labor costs; (e) profitability of facility (the profit goals expected directly affect the pricing of food and beverage); (f) types of purchasing (it is cheaper to purchase in bulk rather than on a charge per person); (g) liquor laws and taxes. It is helpful to the facility staff if you have a history of the amount spent for conferences in catering functions and by attendees at restaurants and room service. They will plan their schedules so that there are sufficient waiters and waitresses during the times your attendees will be eating, resulting in faster service.

As soon as you know your food and beverage needs, call the catering department. They are happy to help you. A good working relationship is important.

Cost-Cutting Ideas for Food Events

- *Do not use the printed menus.* It is not necessary. Instead, give the catering department a budget for your events, and ask them to plan special menus for you. Caterers are creative and can fit your needs.
- *Purchase food in bulk and beverages on a consumption basis.* Many preplanned menus show a cost per person. I have found that most properties are generous with food portions, and there can be wasted food. It is better to buy in bulk. (See section on how much food to order later in the chapter.)
- *Plan receptions in the midmorning or the midafternoon.* It will be cheaper than having a reception over the dinner hour when attendees will use the occasion as their dinner.
- *Use chicken, fish, turkey, or pasta as entrees at luncheons or dinners.* They tend to be less expensive than beef or pork. Many people today are health conscious, and these types of meals fit their lifestyle. Keep luncheons light so that attendees do not feel drowsy for the afternoon sessions. It is helpful if you can print the menus in the publicity. If there is no space for the full menu, at least list the entree, so that people with dietary restrictions can contact you in advance. Most properties are willing to fix a special plate for them. Always reserve a few vegetable or fruit plates.

How Much Food Should Be Ordered?

It is helpful to know how much food to order. It is embarrassing to run out of food, but you also do not want to have a lot of food left over. That is costly. I have one major rule of thumb that I have learned over the years:

Box 6.1

- Order two thirds as much food as you feel you need for your anticipated attendance.
- Learn about your attendees' tastes and order accordingly.

It is very important to call the catering director at the facility. He or she will be very helpful in suggesting menus and quantities. During the event, if you find you are running low on food, the meeting facility generally has a stock of alternative food and beverages that they can bring out within a few minutes.

Record the amount of food you order. It gives you an idea of what to order at your next conference. If your school has sponsored other conferences, use those records as a basis for ordering.

There are charts available that give guidelines for ordering. I will share these with you if you contact me.

Ask the catering staff to vary their food presentations. Creative presentations go a long way toward making a memorable event. If they have decorations left over from previous functions, they may be willing to use it for yours. If you order floral arrangements, ask the banquet staff to keep them for you to be used for other events that you sponsor.

Most university-sponsored conferences will have relatively low budgets, but there are several props that can be used to dress up an event. Think about the purpose of the function and plan the decor and setups accordingly. Hotels generally have a variety of colored table linens. Choose colors that will coordinate with your other decorations. Inexpensive balloons can be used for decorations. Colored leaves can be used very effectively. Mirrors and candles add a nice touch.

The character of the rooms selected to house the events also makes a difference.

Prepare Catering Function
Sheets for the Facility

It is important to have everything planned in great detail for food events. I prepare a catering function chart. Appendix F shows a sample page from my events. Send everything to the catering department whenever menus are finalized. Their staff will carefully read your orders and contact you if they have questions. They may suggest alternative food stretchers to help make the function more effective and save you money. If you have sent diagrams of room setups, they may also make suggestions. They will know if there is not enough space for all you wish to do in the room. After reviewing everything, the catering department will retype your material into *banquet event order (BEO)* sheets translated into language for their staff. Check these carefully against your records to make sure everything corresponds. These are the forms from which the billings for your food and beverages will be generated. If there are questions, call the catering director, and write the changes directly on the form. Initial and date these changes. Keep one copy for yourself for your notebook, and return the other copy to catering. You will need to follow up again once the conference begins.

Secure Entertainment

If you have money in your budget, you may want to bring in entertainment for your networking functions.

There are two important factors that determine what you can provide for entertainment: (a) the preferences of your attendees and (b) your budget.

Here are some guidelines as you begin to plan:

- Ask committee members, some attendees, and the local arrangements committee for ideas and contacts.
- Check with outside sources to see if they are willing to sponsor hospitality events.

- Be sure several people on the committee have seen the acts. Avoid embarrassing situations at the performance. Know your audience! You do not want entertainment that may offend some of the attendees.

- You may wish to have an attorney check the contracts. Be sure that all charges such as honoraria; technical or setup charges for sound, lights, and staging; travel or accommodation costs; and facility costs are included in the contract. Entertainers should *not* be hired as employees.

- If the entertainer has an agent, include a clause in the contract that the agent will be present at the performance with the entertainer. Send the agent complete details on the facility where the performance will be given, including stage diagram, acoustic and other technical information, time of availability for equipment setup and sound check.

- Allow adequate time for setup when scheduling the room. It takes a long time to set all the technical equipment and to rehearse in the facility to adjust sound, lights, and so on.

- Give the conference facility a complete list of the equipment needs such as microphones, lights, staging, power feeds, and a dressing room. The dressing room, if needed, must be reserved in your conference planning schedule.

- Write out guidelines for the entertainer and the agent regarding dialogue with the audience, material you want to have announced, and taboo areas for comedy or songs.

- Ask for a complete media kit so that you can send out accurate publicity.

There is one important element that needs to be checked for entertainment and exhibits: *music licenses*. Each time that a song is performed publicly, U.S. Copyright law demands that permission must be granted, and a royalty fee must be provided to the composer/arranger. There are two performance rights organizations that offer blanket music licensing agreements so that you do not have to ask permission for each song that is performed. Ask the entertainers if they have secured licenses from the American Society of Composers,

Authors and Publishers (ASCAP) and from Broadcast Music Incorporated (BMI). Check out the license agreements before hiring a musician. This is a very controversial issue; call ASCAP and BMI to discuss details of your music. Their addresses and phone numbers are listed in Appendix K.

Four to Six Weeks Before the Conference

If you are using convention bureau or university conference center personnel for registration help, submit your request in writing now: State the number of people you will need, the hours they should work, the type of work they will be doing, and what time and to whom they should report. If you need to rent any equipment for the conference, you should ask about this in your letter. They will give you a list of rental places if they do not have the equipment. The following are some things you might need: a bulletin typewriter (very large type) for typing name badges on-site, other typewriters, computers, and printers. If you are meeting on a campus facility, you may have access to everything; however, if you are off-campus, sometimes it may be necessary to rent these items.

Prepare Room Setup Staging Guide
and Letter of Instructions for the Facility Staff

After you have assigned the meeting space, you are ready to send the conference facility a letter of instructions. My letter outlines the following details:

- List of conference staff, board of directors, and special speakers
- Conference staff responsibilities
- Master account billing instructions
- Special requests

- Special amenities and arrangements for keynote speakers and staff
- Setting up a system of daily contact between facility staff and convention staff
- Information to help the facility have sufficient staff for our needs: times for check-in, checkout, restaurants, and room service
- Telephone system details
- Review of exhibit needs
- General rules for meeting room setups
- General rules for catering functions
- List of keynote speaker and staff sleeping rooms to be placed on the master account, list of charges that are billed to master account, and list of charges that are billed to the individuals
- Other special requests

After the letter is completed, I prepare the staging guide, which contains comprehensive instructions that describe every meeting and event that is scheduled from the beginning to the end of the conference. It is set up in table format. Each event is listed separately. For a sample page from my staging guide, see Appendix G. Although I have a standard form, I check with the hotels and request a copy of their usual function sheets that are given to their staff. I then tailor mine to fit theirs. In the past 3 years, the hotels have used my staging guide exclusively for the NCFR's conferences. They have added a few handwritten notes when necessary. It is easier for everyone to work from the same instructions, and there is less chance for error. Sometimes I include diagrams for specific functions to make sure equipment is placed where it is needed. The diagrams do not have to be professionally drawn.

If you send the staging guide and your letter at least 4 weeks prior to the event, it gives the facility staff time to carefully review everything and call you if there are questions. The fewer last-minute changes that need to be made, the more efficiently the conference will run.

Prepare the Printed Program
and Other Packet Materials

The timing for completion of the final printed program varies. In some associations, the final program is sent several months in advance so that people can carefully review it to plan which sessions to attend. A program supplement listing last-minute changes is included in the registration packets. Other conferences may include only a preliminary program with the advance publicity and distribute the final program at the conference. If there are only a few sessions, some conference planners require registrants to sign up in advance for their choices. Assignments of session rooms are based on attendance. Then the final program is printed at the last minute. Your program committee should decide what is the best method for you.

The printed program should be a comprehensive guide for attendees: an answer sheet for all the questions that will be raised. The cover should list the name of the conference, the dates, the location, the theme (if applicable), and other pertinent information. Include the following in the body of the program: (a) table of contents; (b) general information (hotel and registration forms and information), description of types of sessions, ongoing services, special events, refund procedures, emergency procedures, and so on; (c) complete program schedule including date, day, starting and ending times, name of room, name of session, and listing of presentations and speakers (some conferences have a brief description of the session); (d) index of program participants; (e) map of facility; (f) program at a glance (see Appendix H) if there are many breakout sessions; and (g) other information.

Allow plenty of time when you print the program. If you have university staff at your disposal, they may be able to typeset almost everything on the computer so that there is a minimum of work needed to be done by the printer. This saves a lot of time and money. Have at least three people proofread the copy before it goes to the printer. Ask staff who are not familiar with the conference to read the program book and see if they can understand it. There are many ways to save money and still have an attractive printed program. Ask your printer and staff members with a marketing or graphic arts background for their advice.

Prepare Packet Materials

Most conferences provide a packet of materials that are handed out to arriving registrants. Items that can be included are the printed program (or a supplement with last-minute changes if the program was sent in advance); list of exhibitors (if applicable); list of attendees; information about restaurants, sites, and events in the area; and miscellaneous announcements. For smaller conferences of 30 to 50 people, you may wish to place the name badge, the badge holder, and the tickets in the packets.

It has been my experience that it is cheaper to print all the materials locally before going to the conference: You know the quality of your local printer's work. If you wait until arrival at the conference, you are taking a chance with an unknown company, and the job may cost more. Take the originals of everything you have printed with you to the conference; if something is lost or your attendance swells, you can have your material reprinted there.

At the conferences in which I am involved, registration packets are always prepared before I and my staff go. There is a lot of work in setting up on-site, and it is much easier if this is already done. You need to decide what kind of packet envelopes to use, taking into account your budget. You may be fortunate to secure a sponsor who will provide envelopes or bags.

One to Two Weeks Before the Convention

The conference day is approaching fast. You have accomplished a lot, and now you can concentrate on the last-minute details.

Print Name Badges and Prepare Tickets

There is nothing sweeter in all the earth than the sound of one's own name. Name badges are an important part of a conference because they identify the attendees. This will be one of the last-minute projects, because you want as many as possible printed before you arrive at the conference. Name badges usually have the name of the conference and a logo on the top. The name of the registrant, his or her affiliation, and city and state of residence are typed on the bottom. If possible, try to use large lettering so that names are legible from a distance. There are computer software packages available for name badges, such as PC Nametag, or you may have something set up at your university. If you must do this manually, use a bulletin typewriter with large type. Keep badges filed in alphabetic order. Some conferences separate them by paid and unpaid registrations.

There are many companies that prepare blank name badges and holders. I have found that with my laser printer, I can now have a local quick-print company print the blank name badges with the logo and the name of conference. They perforate the sheets to fit the holders. This saves a lot of money. The badge holders are ordered in large quantities to take advantage of lower prices. If you are having a 1-day conference and you have a low budget, you may want to use press-on badges and have attendees write their own names on them.

If your university has hosted several conferences, you may wish to recognize attendees who are coming for the first time. This can be done either with a different colored name badge, or with a colored sticker attached to the badge. You may also wish to identify the different types of registrants.

After the name badges are printed, thoroughly check the registration forms and assign tickets for special events. Place name badges and tickets in envelopes, filed alphabetically. Sometimes I have special notes and colored ribbons for committee members, and I put these in their envelopes, too.

Pack Supplies

This is probably one of the most dreaded but important jobs in preparing for the conference. Include at the very least the following items:

- Pens
- Sharpened pencils and a sharpener
- Ruler
- Highlighter pens
- Scotch tape
- Thumbtacks
- Stapler and staples
- Liquid Paper
- Envelopes, letterhead, and stamps
- Post-it notes and phone message pads
- Registration packets
- Notebooks and folders
- Battery-operated calculators with extra batteries
- Extension cords and extra bulbs for projectors
- Registration forms from preregistered attendees
- Attendees' envelopes containing name badges, tickets to events, and so on
- Name badge holders
- Plain 8½ in. x 11 in. paper
- Extra registration forms for new people registering on-site
- Membership renewal forms as many people are in the mood to renew while at an association conference

Pack the following supplies for the cashier and/or on-site registration personnel:

- Receipt book and preprinted computer forms
- Equipment for processing charge cards
- Extra programs and other materials for sale
- Extra tickets for all functions

- Envelopes for balancing cash receipts
- Cash box

Pack supplies by areas of use. For example, put all registration materials together in boxes. Keep registration forms in order. Supplies for other staff will be done in the same way. The NCFR has a color coding system for each department. This makes it easier to unpack at the conference. A master control sheet lists each box number. When I and my staff arrive at the conference site, the boxes are all delivered. We check off the boxes to see that they have all arrived and they are then being unpacked.

If you are not transporting materials yourself by car, make arrangements with the conference facility and a shipping company. I have found that the most inexpensive way to ship is by air cargo with a very reasonable convention rate. Everything arrives in 1 to 2 days. You can save a lot of money by taking the boxes directly to the airport rather than using a trucking company to pick up your boxes at the university. One note of caution: Be sure to check out the university's liability policy to see if it covers staff or students driving for the school.

Do *not* ship your box that contains the registration forms, nor the envelopes that contain tickets, name badges, and so on. Bring those with you in a suitcase. This year at the NCFR convention, the airline lost that box, and all the name badges, the receipts, the tickets, and so on had to be redone on-site.

Prepare Instructions
for Helpers and Set Up Meetings

Working at a conference requires a team effort. Each person has important tasks that make everything run smoothly. Divide up the work among all your staff members who are helping at the conference. Some will work in registration; others check name badges or room setups, work in exhibits, accompany keynote speakers, run errands, and so on. Write out comprehensive job descriptions for each person and task. I also set up a time chart of where each person is scheduled each day, which is the guide for our whole staff.

Try to think of all types of questions that could be asked at a conference and have sample answers printed for all staff and volunteers. This is helpful because attendees want their questions answered at the moment, not an hour later.

I usually brief my staff twice before the conference. All last-minute changes are listed in their programs so that everyone is aware of what is happening.

Write Announcements/
Instructions for Session Presiders

If announcements need to be made in sessions, I try to write them in advance and give them to the session presiders. It is also helpful to write out introductions to speakers for the presiders. Try to keep key people such as the program committee members informed.

Make Arrangements
for Hosting Keynote Speakers

It is necessary to arrange for hosts and hostesses to assist with keynote speaker needs. Keynote speakers need to be treated with courtesy and kindness. Taking care of them is important. One year the NCFR had a preconference workshop that had arranged for a well-known person to speak. This committee had not informed the NCFR, nor had they made arrangements to meet the speaker. The speaker drove through a downpour for 45 minutes early in the morning. When he arrived at the hotel, he asked a bellman where he was supposed to speak. None of the hotel staff members had any idea what was going on, so the speaker turned around and went home. This all could have easily been prevented.

It is best if one person is assigned to host each speaker. Ask the speakers for their scheduled arrival and departure dates and the number of nights they will be staying at the conference site. If they are staying overnight, make the reservation in your letter to the facility. After you receive the speaker arrival times, check with your volunteers and make up a schedule for the hosts. The host or hostess should meet the speaker at the airport and see to his or her needs throughout the conference.

If you are having a small conference and are picking up all out-of-town attendees, you may wish to set up a shuttle service or have a team of volunteers. Be sure to let everyone know the arrangements in advance, in writing!

If you have all of these tasks done, you will be ready for the opening of the conference. Chapter 7 will discuss the necessary tasks when you arrive at the conference.

7 | On-Site Conference Logistics

Checklist 7.1

☐ Be prepared!
☐ Arrive early, acquaint yourself with the layout of the facility, unpack boxes, and set up directional signs.
☐ Conduct a preconvention meeting with the facility staff, the event coordinator, and the key program committee or staff *before* the convention begins.
☐ Set up and staff a registration/information area.
☐ Meet daily with the facility staff and the program committee or staff to go over schedule, setups, and questions.
☐ Make yourself available to meet attendees' needs.
☐ Expect the unexpected.
☐ Maintain a sense of humor!

The conference is finally about to begin. You are excited and fearful. It is time for on-site logistics. Everything that is done at the conference is for the sole purpose of helping attendees move directly and efficiently from one place to another to get the most out of their experience. This chapter lists tasks that need to be done. You can then adapt these to your individual situation. Successful conferences, large and small, use the same basic principles; only the amount of work varies.

Be Prepared! Arrive Early and Set Up Everything

I have learned that everything runs more smoothly if you arrive on-site early —*before* everyone else. When I first started working at conferences, I and my staff got to the site the day that registration opened. We then raced to get the boxes open and registration set up. Sometimes our local committees had not stuffed the packets, and we also had to do that (drafting others to help us). By the time we were ready for registration to open, we were exhausted and harried. Now we prepare our packets at our home office, ship them to the conference, and arrive at the site at least 1 day before any part of the conference begins.

Once we are on the premises, we immediately tour the facility, pretending we are attendees coming in for the first time. The staff then knows where every room is located, and we make notes about things that might be confusing to others. One year our hotel had four levels of meeting room space (two were below street level and very difficult to find). We made more signs after we got lost trying to find the meeting rooms that were located below street level. We made color-coded signs almost like "follow the yellow brick road" to find the rooms.

Next, get your boxes unpacked. If your boxes were color-coded and you sent the facility staff instructions on where to deliver the boxes, the job is easy. Take an inventory. If anything is missing, check with the receiving department, and then call the shipping company if it was not found. Then take a look at your inventory sheet, and decide what supplies you may need to purchase and what materials need to be photocopied again.

After sorting, unpack the boxes and set up your office areas. Keep supplies at your fingertips. Mark items that are to be used later in the week with Post-it notes and lay everything out on your worktable. It is important to be well organized at the beginning. Sometimes as the conference reaches fever pitch, you may be running around frantically trying to find something.

Set up signs to make it easier for people to find their way. Ask the facility what types of materials can be used to fasten them. They all want signs to be unobtrusive. If the facility has enough easels, securely tape the signs to them. Check your signs during the conference; sometimes they come loose or are missing.

Try to get everything set up early, before attendees arrive. Keep a small notebook with you and write down any items you need as they come to your mind while unpacking or setting up stations. Try to get a good night's sleep before the conference begins. In the morning, you will feel enthusiastic about getting started.

Conduct a Preconvention Briefing With Facility Staff and Key Program Committee/Staff

One of the most important ways to ensure a successful meeting is to have a preconvention meeting (precon meeting) with the conference chair and other key staff members to meet with the facility coordinators. The purpose of this meeting is to reconfirm arrangements with the facility, the program planning committee, and the staff. It is usually the first time that all parties are together. This meeting sets the tone for the conference and provides last-minute information. Your key committee and staff members will be introduced to the facility staff so that everyone knows each other.

Your staging guide was sent to the facility 1 month before the conference, and its staff has had time to study it carefully. During the precon meeting, details for room setups, food and beverage menus, audiovisual equipment setups, and other areas are reviewed step-by-step. Responsibilities and the channels of communication and authority for emergencies during the conference are defined. Be sure that your instructions on the staging guide match what has been conveyed to the facility staff; ask for copies of all memos that they have circulated to the various departments. Give your programs and agendas to all key service people. When the precon meeting is over, everyone should feel fully informed about what is to happen.

Immediately following this session, the program committee and staff should meet together to review their roles. Let each person voice any concerns so that potential problems can be resolved at this point. Determine how you will communicate with each other throughout the conference.

Setup and Staff Registration/ Information Areas

These areas are the first places toward which attendees gravitate when they arrive. Everything should be set up as efficiently as possible to make it easy for them to register and to obtain answers to their questions. Time is of the essence in registration. Your job is to establish procedures that eliminate any delays. When attendees have quick, positive experiences at registration, they begin the conference on positive, upbeat notes. Conversely, if there is frustration from long lines and unanswered questions, they will be dissatisfied and convey this discontent to others.

As you set up the area, put yourself in the place of the people coming through the registration line. Ask the facility staff to hang your banner so that attendees will see where to register and obtain information. The directional signs that you prepared will enable attendees to easily find their way. If you marked the registration site on a map in the advance materials sent to preregistered attendees, it will simplify things. Between that and the signs, you should be in good shape.

Set up the registration stations. The registration stations can be tables or lighted registration counters rented from a decorating company. The number of stations you set up for each area depends on the size and the complexity of your conference. If your attendance is relatively small, perhaps you can have one person handle preregistered attendees and have another person do on-site registrations. When the numbers go over 100, then a general rule of thumb is: *One station for each 100 people.*

This means that, if you are anticipating 300 people and 100 have registered, you would have one person working on preregistrations and two on on-site registrations. If you expect many on-site registrations, it is helpful to have an additional person typing name badges to keep the traffic flow moving. Obviously, these rules—like others in conference planning—can be broken depending on your situation. For example, at NCFR, 90% of the 1,100 attendees register before the conference, yet there are only three stations for preregistrations and one cashier for on-site registrations the first day. This system works so well for preregistrations that there is minimal work involved. I and my staff also know from past history that people come at a pretty even flow throughout the day, so that it is unnecessary to have more stations. On the other hand, our cashier stays consistently busy with ticket sales and on-site registrations, which take longer.

It is a good idea to use a rope and a stanchion to keep registration lines orderly.

Have one area that says, *Preregistered.* Within this section there will be several stations for attendees who have already registered. Use large signs indicating the alphabetic divisions. Set supplies at each registration station. Start out with a few things, and keep extras nearby in the storage area. Supplies will disappear, and you will need to replenish them throughout the day. It is nice to always be prepared with more than you think you will need. I am always amazed at the

types of materials attendees will want to use during a conference; they are impressed when they ask for something, and
you can provide it.

The second station should have a separate sign, *On-Site
Registration*, for those who have not preregistered.

Set up a separate table where on-site registrants can fill out
the forms before getting in line. The table should be away
from the registration line, but nearby so that it is easy to get
into the line. At this table set up an instructional sign, and
have extra registration forms and pens. Have a low table and
chairs for those who need it and also someone to help the visu-
ally impaired. If there is not enough space in the registration
area for an extra table, provide clipboards at the registration
counters with blank registration forms and a pen attached.

Be sure to post signs with the registration hours so that you
can set up without people interrupting you. One year the
NCFR had a lovely registration area with Dutch doors. This
was nice because when I and my staff were setting up each
morning we could unlock the bottom section of the door,
crawl in and get everything ready behind the scenes. One day
an attendee crawled through the bottom door and called,
"Cindy! I need to talk to you!" This is where a sense of humor
comes in handy.

Set up a message center near the registration area. During
a conference, attendees often receive messages from their
long-lost colleagues, their families, or employers. It is difficult to relay these in person, but a message center can enable
attendees to pick up the messages. Place alphabetical letters
on the board so that messages can be arranged to make them
easier to find.

Additional information tables should be separated from
the registration lines. It is helpful to have a local information
center staffed by people who are familiar with the area so
that attendees can find out about local sites and events. If you
do not have exhibits, it is nice to have a table available for
colleges, universities, and attendees to display pamphlets,
catalogs, and announcements. Some conferences provide

audio- and videotaping services where attendees can purchase these items before they leave the premises. Place these
services in the general registration area, but far enough away
to avoid bottlenecks.

There are no fixed rules for registration. For example, some
conferences prefer to use a computer on-site, whereas others
will use a computer for preregistrations and work from print-
outs, and process on-site registrations by hand. Whichever
method you choose, you must provide a training session for
the registration personnel. Choose these people carefully! If
your conference is small and held at a university conference
center, you may wish to bring some of your staff to assist.
They are usually the ones who processed the preregistrations
and are familiar with the procedures and the names of registrants. This can be an advantage if attendees have questions
about their registration. Sometimes it is necessary to bring in
people who are not familiar with your particular conference
to help. The local convention and visitors bureau has well-
trained, professional, bonded personnel who can assist at a
nominal fee. Their staff have excellent rapport with attendees. You must submit a written request to them 4 to 6 weeks
before the conference. Student volunteers are also usually
excellent as registration clerks. They are bright, eager to meet
people, and enjoy helping to make conferences run well—
and they also get free registration. They are very helpful to
those attending the conference for the first time. It is generally easy to find student volunteers. In your advance publicity, you can write an article requesting volunteers. You can
also contact graduate departments of universities.

Write explicit instructions for those who work in registration. Include items such as how to fill out forms, policies for
problem solving, how to type name badges, who is authorized
to collect money, and how to answer commonly asked questions. Hand these instructions out in advance so that workers
are familiar with the procedures. Set up a training session at
least 20 minutes before registration begins. Introduce the staff
who will be available to handle problems.

Registration Procedures

All stations should be set up a minimum of 30 minutes before registration opens. Make sure packets and other supplies are replenished. Try to have extra volunteers who can check the registration stations periodically so that there will be no delays because you ran out of something. Do not wait until the last minute to get set up.

Preregistered

If you are prepared, this should be simple. The attendee's name is checked off on a registration printout. He or she is handed the registration packet, a name tag, tickets to special events, and a name badge holder. The person is on his or her way in about 1 minute.

If an attendee has to pay more money or needs special assistance, he or she is sent to a separate line for resolution. In this case, the name badge and packets are not given to the registrant until after everything is settled with the cashier.

On-Site Registration

Give the cashier written instructions regarding balancing paper work with accumulated cash and checks.

In a separate line, new registrants need to fill out the registration form and pay the appropriate amount. Prepare a receipt, either by hand or with the computer. Give one copy to the attendee and keep a duplicate for your records. Type up a name badge and give the receipt, a packet, and tickets (if the registrant signed up for special events) to the person.

The worst fear for registration personnel is having an unhappy attendee with a complaint who wants to voice it now. One rule of thumb for solving this type of problem is the following: Ask the attendee how he or she would like to handle the problem, then resolve the issues back at your office rather than holding up the registration line and making others feel uncomfortable. Take down all important information, soothe or apologize to the person, issue him or her a name badge, and check when you get back to your office.

Hold to your scheduled registration hours. At the end of each registration period, set out a sign with the hours posted, and encourage people to return the next time registration is open.

At the close of registration, count cash, balance out, and take the money to a safe-deposit box. It is best to have someone accompany the cashier. If the registration area is open, supplies will need to be moved to a locked area; if you are fortunate to have a locked prefunction area, you can secure and set up all stations for the next time. It is helpful to prepare everything for the next day, even if you must move supplies. The next morning you will be glad you did.

Communicate Daily
With the Convention and Facility Staff

There is a universal rule of conferences: Things will come up that are unplanned. For this reason it is important to keep in close contact with all people involved. Keep in touch with staff and volunteers through daily memos or meeting personally. One of the NCFR's staff members once suggested to use the registration area as the central location for leaving memos. Even if staff members do not see each other, they can still pass the information.

Keep a Close Watch on
Setups and Food Functions

If everything was planned in advance, a major task on-site is to double- and triple-check all setups so that every event is ready to start on time and will run smoothly.

The conference chair oversees these details and can assign other staff members to help with the checking. Make sure you have a list of phone numbers of all facility people you might need to call in the event of last-minute changes or emergencies. Sometimes the facility will provide the conference chair with a pager or walkie-talkie to be in immediate contact, but at least, the facility staff should be accessible by phone.

Arrange to meet with catering staff once or twice a day to update them on numbers and to check menus. Before you meet, check with your registration staff to see if additional tickets have been sold. Then update your count for catering.

Give the hotel staff a list of your key people who are authorized to make changes in room arrangements and approve food function sheets. Instruct them that, if attendees or program presenters want to change the room setups or order additional food, they are to call you immediately. In some facilities, even the simple request to move chairs can result in excessive charges to you, so you and some of your key people need to maintain control over orders and expenses.

Another key task is an early morning walk-through of the facility with the head of the convention service setups. I usually begin at 6:00 a.m. when very few people are around. During this time, I check all room setups, note any changes needing to be made, and look at the overall appearance of the facility.

Approximately 30 minutes before sessions are scheduled to begin, check with the leaders and presenters to see if everything is set. If audiovisual equipment has been ordered, make sure it is in the room and running. It can be advantageous to hire experts to handle this portion of the conference, especially if your knowledge of equipment is minimal. Many speakers today require sophisticated equipment, which must be working for a successful presentation.

Oversight of food functions begins a minimum of 60 minutes before the scheduled event. Look at the general room setup and the proper number of tables and chairs, and glance at the table settings. Visit with the wait staff to determine the progress of the food and whether everything will be ready on time. If writing materials need to be placed at the tables, do it early so that you will not interfere with the facility staff setting up. Meet with the banquet captain and learn his or her schedule so you can easily reach him or her if more food is needed. Be sure to advise the captain of any change in number of participants. During the event, keep an eye on the food and replenish, if necessary. After the session, check on any unopened beverages you purchased by the bottle, because these can usually be deducted from your bill.

Note the attendance at all sessions. Student volunteers enjoy doing this because they can also listen to some of the sessions. Put these records in your notebook with other statistics. Session attendance indicates the interests of attendees and will help you decide the program for future conferences.

Make Yourself Available
to Meet Attendees' Needs

After everything has been checked and is running smoothly, it is important to visit some of the sessions. Talk with attendees in the hallways, and ask if there is anything they need. Helping other people at conferences has been a real joy to me. It is wonderful to see smiles on faces.

Expect the Unexpected,
Be Prepared for Emergencies

The last thing you must remember is that things may not always go smoothly, even if you are well prepared. Be ready to think on your feet. Sometimes a speaker fails to arrive because of a family emergency, and you need to find a substitute. A meeting room may have to be switched because the facility made an error and scheduled two events in the same room at the same time. You may have to make a quick sign and post someone at the original room to tell people the new location. These may be trying times, so I use a sense of humor and keep things in perspective. Be prepared for medical emergencies. In all the years I have been planning conferences, I have been fortunate to have had only one medical emergency; however, you need to have a system in place. Before coming to the conference, compile a list of names, addresses, and phone numbers of the police, the fire department, the ambulance, and the nearby hospitals. Familiarize yourself with the facility's policies for emergencies to ensure that if there is a crisis it can be handled smoothly. It probably is not necessary to perform cardiopulmonary resuscitation (CPR), but you need to know what to do and whom to contact to get immediate attention. Ask the facility about who is responsible for transporting family members to and from the hospital if someone is taken there on a medical emergency. Determine who will contact family members back home. Check with the airlines about their bereavement and emergency policies so that you can share this information with attendees if necessary. Also record your staff members' medical insurance carriers and family members to contact for emergencies.

Years ago, someone told me that the secret to a successful conference is that, if mistakes happen, you can fix the problems with very few people knowing that anything went wrong. At one of the Minnesota Christian Convention's conferences, four of us arrived at 6:00 a.m. to check on a function for 400 people that was scheduled to begin at 7:00 a.m. The hotel had my staging guide in advance, and I had discussed everything with them the day before. That morning there was seating for *100* people, and there was only one person working! We quickly helped move chairs and tables, pull Danish out of the oven, mix juice, put coffee in pots, carry serving trays, and so on. By 7:00 a.m., we were ready for all 400 people, and no one knew what had happened except for the hotel staff and the four of us. The hotel apologized for its error. They learned to heed what meeting planners tell them.

If you are ready to respond quickly to these situations, everything will run smoothly, and you will feel a great sense of accomplishment. After the conference is over, you are ready to begin the last phase of planning: evaluation and follow-up. Chapter 8 will talk about the importance of these tasks.

8 | Postconference Activities

Checklist 8.1

☐ Prepare to ship materials from the conference site.
☐ Decide on gratuities for conference facility staff.
☐ Check master account billing for accuracy. Write down what each item is on the bill *before* you leave.
☐ Conduct debriefing meetings with facility staff, program committee, and staff.
☐ Summarize the conference evaluations completed by attendees; evaluate which suggestions should be incorporated into planning of future conferences.

The conference program is over, and most of the attendees have gone home. People complimented you about the great meeting, how well organized you and the committee were, and about the valuable information they learned. You are feeling on top of the world! However, there are some items that need your attention before you can say this conference is finished.

Prepare to Ship Materials
From the Conference Site

It is tempting to just throw things into boxes, thinking you can sort after you are back at the office. At this point, you are tired and want to get everything out of the way so that you can go home. I have learned, however, that once the materials are back at the office I am not in the mood to sort. What usually happens is that, unless the supplies are used every day in the office, the box gets put on the shelf, and nothing happens until the next conference. Try to discipline yourself to pack it right, even if you are taking the materials by car. It makes it easier to find everything when you unpack at the office. Use the same methods you used to pack in preparation for the conference.

Decide on Gratuities
for Conference Center Service Staff

One of the most difficult decisions to make concerns gratuities. This is left to the discretion of the conference sponsor. In some facilities, the gratuity may be included in the total package price, eliminating extra tipping. Most facilities build in gratuities for food functions. At many facilities, there are especially helpful staff members who should be thanked for their services with additional gratuities. Think about the following when you decide whom and how much to tip:

- People to whom you should remember to give gratuities: luggage handlers, bus and taxi drivers, escorts, hosts, doormen, bell staff, room attendants, captains, wait staff, bartenders, room service waiters, wine stewards, chef and staff, setup crews, cartage people, cleanup crew. Ask the facility director for its policies on tipping. If they charge a fee per box for moving boxes, you may not have to add gratuity for these people.

- Ask the facility about the preferred method of distribution: Specify amounts for each person, or give a lump sum to the convention service person to distribute equitably.
- A general rule of thumb is to calculate gratuities based on 1% to 1 ½% of the total bill, depending on the number of food and beverage functions, the complexity of setups, and the extra demands on service personnel.

Leave the gratuity in cash, with a list of the people who have provided exceptional service for you. Give it to the facility director to take care of the distribution. Keep accurate records of the name of recipients, the nature and amount of gratuities, and the receipts in the event the Internal Revenue Service (IRS) asks for proof that you actually distributed the gratuity.

Check the Master Account Billing for Accuracy

It is important to keep an eagle eye on the master account at the facility. This is the billing for everything that is being charged to you. In the hotel staging guide, I always specify a preferred way of setting up the billing for easier verification. Each facility has its own accounting method, and no two billings will ever look the same. Usually, the master account has a summary of items billed, followed by copies of backup material so that you can see everything that has transpired. I ask for charges for food functions, sleeping room charges for the people who are placed on the master account, audiovisual equipment charges, and charges for miscellaneous items to be separated to make it easier to check. Each day of the conference, I try to glance at the billing to see if all the charges are correct. On the last day of the conference I go over everything in detail.

Check all charges and the corresponding backup. Compare these with the banquet event orders and the staging guide that you sent before the conference. Check the quantities of food on the bill in relationship to what you originally ordered. Write identifiers on the backup paperwork so that you know exactly what you are being charged for.

As you check over your account look to see who signed the paperwork. Sometimes unauthorized charges show up on the bill. These need to be questioned immediately. Ask the accounting staff to explain them, and if adjustments need to be made, give them in writing to the proper person. There will be some charges that have not been posted by the last day. The final master account bill is usually sent 7 to 10 days after the conference. When this comes, compare it with the bill you received before you left the property.

Conduct an Evaluation Meeting With Facility Staff Before Leaving the Conference

Before leaving the conference, set up an evaluation meeting with the facility staff. Try to have their setup coordinator, their other key people, and your key conference staff there. It is an effective tool for future conferences. The facility staff will give their perceptions of how everything went and give positive suggestions for improving your next conference. The conference staff in turn can also give its observations. If the meeting is conducted in a positive tone, everyone benefits. The objective of the meeting is to find out how everyone performed, not to complain and point fingers. I have seen hotels change some of their policies after we made suggestions at postconference evaluation meetings. In turn, I have also changed my staging guide several times after seeing how some hotels communicate to their staff. I have also made adjustments in some of the NCFR's registration procedures after a hotel staff gave observations based on other conferences. There is never a perfect conference, and everybody can benefit from constructive dialogue. Be sure to thank the facility staff for their part in making the conference a success.

After you return home, send written thank-you notes to the key facility people, with copies to their supervisors.

Summarize Conference Evaluations

Effective evaluation of the conference is useful for planning future conferences. It is best to evaluate the meeting while everything is fresh in your mind. The basic question that needs to be answered is, Did the conference fulfill everyone's needs? There are different expectations from various people: For you and the planning committee, the main goal was a smoothly run meeting that was well organized and without problems. Attendees want to be challenged with a high-quality program at a reasonable price in pleasant surroundings. Your university may want a conference that will highlight its programs and ultimately result in increased visibility or enrollment. Speakers also appreciate feedback. It is a good idea to have attendees, speakers, planners, and staff all evaluate the conference.

One of the best ways to evaluate is to prepare a form that covers all areas of the conference. If you have regularly scheduled conferences, or similar types of conferences, try to use the same basic form, adapted for each meeting to provide a basis for comparison.

Have specific goals in mind as you draw up the questionnaire. Try to answer the following questions through the form:

1. Did this meeting accomplish its objectives?
2. Was the conference cost-effective?
3. What did the attendees really get out of the meeting?
4. How can we do a better job and spend less next time?

Be sure to also include the following questions on the form:

1. What did attendees think about the conference dates?
2. Did they like the length of the conference?

3. How were session lengths? Too long? Too Short? Just right?
4. Do plans need to be changed for future conferences?

John H. Seeley (1985) suggests that an evaluation should include the tough questions; you should also try to find out your *need*-to-know information, not just nice-to-know information. He also thinks it is important when you write up the evaluations to report in a way that speaks to the key audience; do it soon after the conference, and show actions that can be taken for improvement.

It can be useful to evaluate conference speakers, but sometimes attendees are reluctant to complete evaluations on individuals. If speakers are evaluated, this information should be shared with them in a positive manner to help them in future speaking engagements. I know of one conference that evaluates all its speakers, and the final question is, Would you like to have this speaker return? They want to be sure that only top-notch speakers are selected.

Try to determine the best way to distribute evaluation forms: in registration packets, at sessions, or at the close of the conference. Usually, there is better response if people are reminded about the evaluations verbally during sessions. Some conferences award an incentive prize for those who fill out the forms. Remember that timing affects the responses. If they are given at the end of the conference, there is a halo effect. At the end of sessions, there will be reaction to the presenters. If they are handed to those leaving early, it is not uppermost on their mind, but if they are returned days or weeks later, there is reduced recall.

In my experience, only about 10% of the attendees will fill out a form, and fewer than that if they have to do a lot of writing. Try to have questions that can be answered with yes or no, or by circling choices. Attendees also prefer being offered a range of answers for each question: strongly dislike, moderately dislike, moderately like, strongly like, and so on. If people have complaints about a meeting, they will fill out the evaluations; the majority of those who are satisfied may never fill them out.

Sometimes it is advantageous to hire an unbiased party to summarize the evaluations. Determine if formal or informal analysis is needed, if a narrative is needed for qualitative data. Use care if you are preparing statistics for quantitative data.

After evaluations are summarized, compare the summary with that of other conferences, and see if you can determine trends.

Meet With the Planning Committee and/or Staff for Debriefing

Try to schedule this meeting soon after the conference while everyone can remember details. Before this meeting, each person should write his or her own observations. Try to remember what attendees said about the conference in the hallways, and note this in your own summary.

It is helpful if there is an outline for each person to follow. Typical areas to evaluate in this meeting are the following:

- Meeting site and facilities
- Exhibit program (if applicable)
- Entertainment
- Food and beverage events
- Vendors (if applicable)
- Attendee turnout
- Facility staff
- On-site logistics
- Advance preparations
- Program schedule
- Speakers
- Publicity

If possible, distribute the summary of attendees' evaluations prior to the meeting so that the committee members have time to think about this before discussing everything as a group.

When the meeting convenes, be sure to begin on a positive note and thank everyone for all the hard work. Provide feedback opportunities. Give everyone a chance to speak before discussing the attendee evaluations. When these are brought up, try to determine which suggestions should be incorporated into the next conference and which may be groundless complaints. Wrapping up the conference can be almost as much work as preparing it, but as you thoroughly evaluate the past efforts, planning for the next meeting becomes much easier. After the meeting is over have someone compile a written summary. Include suggestions for the next year.

The conference chair has one last task before putting the meeting to bed: to collect important statistics. Ask the facility to give the following information when the final master account billing is sent: How many attendees actually claimed their reservations? What was the percentage of no-shows? How many rooms were singles, doubles, suites? Check on the usage and gross revenue of the facility's outlets (restaurants, lounges, and room service) from your attendees. They can get this information by calculating from those who charge the meals to their rooms. Ask for the gross sleeping room revenue from your conference block of rooms. The master account does not get paid until this information is provided. I put this information into a chart and give it to the hotels where the NCFR considers holding future conferences. With definite figures, it is easy to calculate the number of rooms that should be blocked, and the hotels can make realistic projections of revenue that they can expect from the next conference.

After the property information is sent, break down conference registration attendance by categories: preregistered versus on-site registrations. When you calculate the number of on-site registrations by day, you can better plan for registration personnel at the next conference. To calculate a no-show percentage, check your actual attendance at conference food functions against the guaranteed numbers. This will help you in determining guarantees for the next conference; perhaps you can cut down on the amount of food ordered.

Next, analyze your budget. Determine which specific areas need to be carefully rebudgeted for future conferences.

After collecting statistics, chart them so that you can keep them in your notebook and use them for reference when you begin the planning process for the next conference. See Appendix I for a sample of a financial impact record.

Finish writing thank-you notes to your staff, program committee, and all others who helped with the conference.

Now you can close the books on this conference. In the introduction, I referred to the planning process as being a giant puzzle. As you have read the book you have been able to see how the pieces fit together.

The first step was to look at how to get the most from a professional conference from the attendees' perspective so that you could plan for their needs. The next step was to design your overall meeting plan, to build a calendar of deadlines, to select a place to hold the conference, and to prepare a budget so that you could determine how much to charge for registration.

The planning then proceeded with preparing the program schedule, selecting the meeting rooms, and marketing the conference to the best audiences.

Following the calendar of deadlines, you and the planning committee prepared for the other conference activities: registration, food functions, meeting room setups, child-care options, signs, registration packets and name badges, assignments for convention personnel, and arrangements to pick up keynote speakers.

As the convention began, you and your staff arrived early to set up registration and signs, met with the facility and convention staff, checked and rechecked all meeting room setups and food functions, and tried to be available to meet attendees' needs.

When the conference was over, you and your committee and staff packed up supplies, met with the facility staff, checked the master account and all other bills, wrote thank-you notes, and evaluated the conference.

After 25 years, I am still excited about planning conferences. I believe that you, too, will feel a great deal of satisfaction when you plan meetings, because meetings provide some of the best opportunities for academics to continue satisfying their thirst for knowledge that is, in turn, passed on to their students.

Because of its length, this book cannot answer all your questions, but I hope it has given you the tools and the references you need to feel ready to tackle this avenue of service in your career. Good luck in your planning!

Sample Job Descriptions

Program Vice President-Elect

1. Attend Program Committee Meetings.
2. Choose the conference theme (to be approved by the board).
   a. Select theme from topics frequently discussed by the media and the public, studied in research and applied fields, and of interest in the city/state/region where the conference will be held.
   b. Submit a written report to the board for its April 22, 1993 meeting, introducing the theme.
3. Select plenary speakers for the conference (summer of 1993).
   a. Solicit ideas from NCFR members and 1994 Program Committee.
   b. Write speaker criteria.
   c. Consult with the conference coordinator and the executive director regarding speaker honoraria.
   d. Send a letter to speakers outlining honoraria, expenses to be covered, conference theme, and speech schedule.
4. Prepare the "Call for Abstracts" with the conference coordinator.
   a. Determine program formats and prepare definitions.
   b. Write general rules for submissions.
   c. Prepare a brief overview of the conference theme.

d. Contact committee members for their guidelines regarding the theme. Ask them to respond by September 1, 1993.

e. Prepare the submission form and the subject categories.

5. Write articles for *NCFR Report*. Deadlines: July 15, November 15, February 15, and May 15.

Audiovisual Equipment Chair

1. Obtain audiovisual equipment locally. Contact area universities, schools, churches, or family service agencies to see if their equipment may be borrowed.

2. The conference coordinator will send a list of equipment needed to be borrowed/rented by September 1, 1993.

   a. Arrange for pickup and return of borrowed equipment. The conference has adequate insurance to cover any damage and/or loss of equipment.

   b. Prepare a list of rented equipment and mark each piece so it is easily distinguishable.

   c. Deliver borrowed equipment to the audiovisual storage area. The audiovisual coordinator will check in the equipment.

   d. If equipment cannot be borrowed, it must be rented locally. Obtain bids from several companies. Give recommendations to the conference coordinator. Together they determine what equipment will be rented. Send all contracts to the executive director for signing.

3. Check daily with the audiovisual coordinator to see if assistance is needed in moving equipment to/from meeting rooms.

4. After the conference, return any equipment that was rented.

Speaker Contract for 1993 Minnesota Christian Convention (March 26-27, Thunderbird Hotel, Bloomington, MN)

Theme: Restoring the Family of God

Name of Speaker:

Address:

Phone (include area code):

Terms of Agreement

1. Honorarium: $ _____.
2. The Minnesota Christian Convention will purchase your plane tickets. Please send your preferred travel times and airline preference to Cindy Winter by January 1, 1993. The tickets will be sent directly to you at the above address from the airline. Preferably, you will be able to stay over Saturday night, March 27, 1993, to *save* on airfare. Someone from the Convention Committee will pick you up at the airport; we will contact you at a later date with the details.
3. You will stay at the Thunderbird Hotel in Bloomington on Friday evening, March 26. Cynthia Winter will make hotel arrangements. The reservation will be held in your name. If you wish, a late checkout can be arranged on Saturday. Please let us know if you would like this service.

4. Meals for Friday evening and Saturday will be covered by the Minnesota Christian Convention. Please let us know if you would prefer to have someone accompany you to dinner on Friday evening, or if you would rather have room service.
5. Times you will be speaking during the convention:
   a. Friday, at 7:30 p.m. (45 minutes).
      Title of talk:
      25-word synopsis of talk:
   b. Continue with other sessions.
6. Please send a biographical sketch, a photo, and if possible, a videotape with a portion of one of your talks to Cindy Winter by October 31, 1992 for advance publicity materials.
7. Audiovisual equipment needed: _____
8. I give permission to the Minnesota Christian Convention to reproduce my presentations in whole or in part, and in any and all forms or media as may be chosen for promotional purposes and for distribution to convention attendees.

We agree to the above conditions.
Name: _____   Name: _____
Speaker   Cynthia Winter,
                             Executive Coordinator
Date: _____   Date: _____

Sample Site Prospectus (Adapted From NCFR Program Specifications)

The Organization

The National Council on Family Relations (NCFR) is a member-funded, nonprofit educational and resource organization. The NCFR (a) provides a forum for family life researchers, educators, and practitioners to share in the development and dissemination of knowledge about families and family relationships; (b) establishes professional standards; and (c) works to promote family policies to enhance family well-being.

The annual conference implements the NCFR's mission by promoting cutting edge research, policy agendas, and networking opportunities for multidisciplinary professionals who deliver services to families. Approximately 1,200 professionals and graduate students attend the conference.

Objectives of the NCFR Annual Conference

- To provide a means for professionals to disseminate cutting edge research and policy information in the diverse fields of the family
- To enable attendees the opportunity to network with leading professionals in the family field

- To share stimulating presentations in varied formats to provide professional development research opportunities
- To offer attendees continuing education credits
- To present the latest audiovisual materials in the family field in exhibits and film screenings
- To give members of the NCFR an opportunity to learn more about the governance of the organization and to provide opportunities for involvement in various conference activities
- To provide a forum for public policy discussion

The NCFR is currently soliciting information for sites to host the 1997, 1998, and 1999 annual conferences. Decisions will be made by December 31, 1993.

Preferred Dates for a Conference

- First 2 weeks in November. The NCFR is fairly flexible within this time frame.
- Days of week: Preconference workshops on Tuesday and Wednesday; conference beginning Thursday morning and concluding on Sunday. The NCFR can be flexible as long as the conference can meet over a weekend for attendees to use lowest airfares.
- The primary determining factor of the city and hotel site (if it has sufficient meeting room space) will be sleeping room rates offered by the hotel for quality service. Other factors include the following: (a) availability of air transportation; (b) location of hotel in downtown area within walking distance from restaurants, shops, cultural events; (c) number of members living in the state who can provide local volunteer support; (d) features of the city.

General Meeting Room Requirements

- A large registration area, preferably close to exhibits and the meeting room area.

- 8,000 sq. ft. to 10,000 sq. ft. for exhibit space and poster sessions. Must be in a locked room, preferably in a section of the ballroom, adjacent to registration and major meeting space (30 8' x 10' booths; the remainder of exhibits are for combined book titles and 4' x 8' poster boards).
- 1 room (8,000 sq. ft. to 10,000 sq. ft.) for general plenary sessions (theater style).
- 9 to 10 rooms for concurrent sessions (varying in size from 500 sq. ft. to 1,500 sq. ft.).
- 2 to 3 rooms (each approximately 500 sq. ft.) for storage of registration and audiovisual supplies and the convention office. All these rooms must be locked 24 hours a day.
- 4 rooms (each approximately 400 sq. ft. to 500 sq. ft.) for ongoing events: press room, employment service, hospitality room, video festival.

Meeting Room Needs
to Be Broken Down by Day

Days 1 and 2 (Tuesday and Wednesday if preferred pattern of Tuesday–Sunday is used): preconference workshops and committee meetings

- 2 to 3 rooms (each approximately 500 sq. ft.) for storage and convention office (24 hours).
- 3 rooms (each approximately 1,000 sq. ft. to 1,200 sq. ft.) for workshops (12:00 p.m. to 5:30 p.m.). Theater style.

Days 3, 4, 5, 6 (Thursday, Friday, Saturday, Sunday): official conference

- Registration area ready to begin at 8:00 a.m. (24 hours).
- Same rooms for ongoing events and storage (24 hours).
- 9 to 10 rooms (ranging from 500 sq. ft. to 1,300 sq. ft.) for concurrent breakout sessions (7:00 a.m. to 6:00 p.m.). Theater style. Four to five rooms will continue until 10:00 p.m.
- 1 room (approximately 800 sq. ft. to 1,000 sq. ft.) for plenary session (two to three 1 ½ hour slots during the day). Theater style. (On Day 4, this room will be needed from 8:30 p.m. to 12:30 a.m. for a dance/party.) If this space is

flexible such as a ballroom, it can be used for the concurrent breakouts.
- Exhibit/poster area (approximately 10,000 sq. ft.) for Days 3, 4, and 5 (24 hours).

Sleeping Room Requirements

Sleeping Room Block Needs

450 rooms for peak night
35 triple/quads exclusively for graduate students
5 rooms for staff (reduced rate below the convention rate)
1 large suite comped above the 1/50 block for president
1 one-bedroom suite for executive director (large table seating 8 to 10 people in the parlor)

Group revenue impact reports are attached.

Sleeping Room Occupancy Pattern

Averages 63% double and 37% single. No show rate for room reservations versus rooms used: 8% average.

Sleeping Room Block Requirements by Day

Day of Week	Room Block Needed for 1997/ 1998/1999	Actual Rooms Used 1992	Actual Rooms Used 1991	Average Occupancy 1987-1990
1 (Monday on preferred pattern)	50	70	40	57
2 (Tuesday)	250	155	190	204
Continue throughout the week Total room nights	1,800	3,005	2,150	1,925

Sleeping Room Rates Requested

The NCFR requests a discounted convention rate of 30% to 40% below rack rate with a sentence included in the contract stating that sleeping room rates will not increase over 6% per year; negotiated 18 months prior to the conference. Approximately 75% of conference attendees pay their own expenses to come to our conferences. Because of this factor, low to moderate sleeping room rates are a *must* for conferences.

History of Sleeping Room Rates

Rate	Hotel and City	Year
$00 S/D (guaranteed)	Hyatt Regency Crown Center, Kansas City, MO	1996
$00 S/$000 D (1991 base price)	Portland Hilton Hotel, Portland, OR	1995
$00 S/D (maximum)	Minneapolis Hilton & Towers, Minneapolis, MN	1994

Current and Past Conference Sites

Year	Convention Dates	Hotel and City
1994	November 8-13	Minneapolis Hilton & Towers, Minneapolis, MN
1993	November 10-15	Hyatt Regency Hotel, Baltimore, MD
1992	November 5-10	Clarion Plaza Hotel, Orlando, FL

Catering Functions for Conferences

- *Snack bar on consignment or take-out deli* (times to be determined): coffee, juice, and danish for breakfast; coffee, soft drinks, fruit, sandwiches, dry snacks, cookies, and so on for lunch. Average daily gross sales: $000. Note: The service is discontinued if sales are insufficient.
- *Major reception* (second day of conference): one cash bar, appetizers for 500 people.

- *Reception(s) for workshop:* one cash bar, appetizers for 175 to 200 people.

Preliminary Hotel Information
Prior to Site Inspection

Please fill out the following information at the time of the site inspection. Send this form to Cynthia Winter, CMP, NCFR, 3989 Central Ave. NE, Suite 550, Minneapolis, MN 55421 (Phone: 612-781-9331; fax: 612-781-9348).

Available dates for conference: _____

Are these dates first or second option: _____

Approximate group sleeping room rates (1993 prices): _____

Number of sleeping rooms available for our block: _____

Other meetings booked prior to, during, or after our conference
with these dates: _____

Complimentary room policy: _____

Suites offered over and above the complimentary ratio: _____

Have you tentatively blocked these dates in the hotel function
book, and if so, how long will you keep these dates open for
the National Council on Family Relations (NCFR)? _____

Hotel rep for NCFR to contact (include name and phone number):

_____

Sample Questionnaire

Answers may be written next to the question on this sheet. This questionnaire will be appended to the hotel contract.

Contracts

1. Does your city and state have a history of equal rights/affirmative action policies? Are there political issues regarding human rights that may later surface?

2.

   a. Is your facility an affirmative action/equal opportunity employer?

b. What policies do you employ to assure that all guests and conference attendees are treated equally with respect and fairness regardless of race, creed, color, or political beliefs?

3.

a. Is your facility union operated?

b. If yes, do you have exclusive union contracts and with which unions?

c. When are present union contracts expiring?

d. Is there a union steward located on the hotel premises?

e. In the event of a strike, what is the hotel's contingency plan for ensuring that the convention would run smoothly in setting up meeting rooms, serving meals, cleaning rooms, and so on?

4. What is your cancellation clause in the event of a political strike, acts of God, or other events that could prevent the NCFR conference from meeting in your facility?

Meeting Rooms

1. Please indicate meeting rooms that are adjacent to restaurants, lounges, pool area, and other recreational facilities that could interfere with educational sessions scheduled in these rooms.

2.

a. When do you need our program? The final program?

b. We assume that once the contract has been signed the hotel will release *no* meeting room space until the final program is given to you, unless the conference coordinator and/or the executive director are consulted.

Sample Program Schedule
Based on 1993 Program

(Note: Rooms are set theater style; use a 10′ per person formula to include a head table for six and any small audiovisual equipment. * Indicates food or beverages will be served.)

Wednesday, November 10, 1993

8:00 a.m. to 9:00 a.m.: Precon meeting (conference and hotel staff) (Hollow square for 20 to 30 people)

8:00 a.m. to 5:30 p.m.: Preconference Workshop on Military Families (1 room approximately 3,500 sq. ft., theater style for main sessions; and 3 additional breakout rooms each approximately 1,000 sq. ft., all set theater style)

10:00 a.m. to 6:00 p.m.: *Certification Review Committee (CRC) meeting (1 room, hollow-square style for 10 people)

Comparison of Sites

Name of City	Hotels	Average 1992 Sleeping Room Rates*	Availability of Air Transportation	Strength of[a] Affiliated Council	Nearby Sites	Notes
Pittsburgh, PA	3 that will fit NCFR. Hilton has blocked Nov. 12-17, 1997.	$88 Single $98 Double	USAir Hub; brand new state of the art airport opened in October; serviced by American, Continental, Delta, Northwest, TWA, United	PA/DE Council strong.	New Carnegie Science Center; Mt. Washington; riverboats; Point State Park; Oxford, Mellon and PPG Centers; historical museum and park across the street from the Hilton Hotel; Heinz Hall; Fountain at the Point; Fifth Avenue Place; Market Square; Subway Station; Pittsburgh Symphony; ballet; Shakespeare theater company; opera; civic light opera; good shopping.	Downtown has been renovated, and is a beautiful city with many fountains, shops, restaurants. In 1985 Rand McNally named city as America's Most Livable City. No steel mills are left in the city.
Rochester, NY	Hyatt Regency has Nov. 3-9 or 10-16. 2 other hotels.	$89 Single or Double	Serviced by American, Continental, Delta, Northwest, United, USAir	New York Council is strong; there are several members in that area.	Shopping; restaurants; historical sites; modern financial district; canals; city waterfalls; parks; museums; Victorian neighborhoods; Performing arts groups.	The Convention and Visitors Bureau is doing a lot of publicity to promote their city.
Syracuse, NY	1	$80s Single $90s Double	American, Continental, Delta, Northwest, TWA, United, USAir	Several members in Syracuse; see above.	Burnett Park Zoo; Discovery Center of Science and Technology; Erie Canal Museum; Onondaga Historical Association; Art museums; Famous Artists Series; Salt City Center for the Performing Arts; Syracuse Area Landmark Theater; Symphony; Opera; Theater Company all in downtown area.	
Philadel- phia, PA	4	High $90s to Low $100s for Singles; Low $100s to $115 for Doubles.	Major airport; most carriers have good connections.	PA/DE Council strong.	Many historical sites; lots of shopping from City Hall to Independence Mall; Market Street East is historical and commercial hub; Wanamakers Department Store; Mellon Independence Hall; many restaurants; Philadelphia Orchestra; ballet; museums.	A new Marriott is being built in downtown Philly which will bring competition to the downtown hotels.

APPENDIX E

Room/Time Chart

Room	10 am	12 pm	1:30 pm	2 pm	3:30 pm	4 pm	5 pm	7:30 pm	8 pm
Ballroom A									
Ballroom B									
Ballroom C									TCRM 7
Ballroom D		TCRM Registration	TCRM 1		TCRM 4				
Ballroom E		TCRM Registration	TCRM 2		TCRM 5				
Ballroom F			TCRM 3		TCRM 6				
Baltimore				Extension Family Life Specialists Workshop					
Annapolis									
Frederick									
Columbia									
Harborview									
Chesapeake A									
Chesapeake B									
Exec. Bd. Rm.				CRC Committee Meeting					Storage
Charles					Storage				
Calvert						Hospitality Room			
Pratt									
Lombard							AC Exec. Com. Mtg.		
Camden									
Douglass						Finance Comm. Mtg.			
Suite 1445/47								92/93 Executive Com. Mtg.	

APPENDIX F

Food and Beverage Function Sheet

Room	Function Name and Set-up	Menu	AV Required
Executive Board Room	CRC Committee Meeting Existing set-up. Bring in buffet cart with food.	High Tech Continenal Breakfast for 7 ppl.	
Ballroom Foyer (outside D, E, and F)	Theory Construction and Research Methodology Workshop Break 2 Serpentine food stations. Please have sign that says "Private Function".	2 gallons coffee 1 gallon decaf 1 gallon hot water (for tea & hot chocolate) 100 assorted soft drinks (use a variety of colas, diet colas, caffeine-free colas, caffeine-free diet colas, and non-colas such as Sprite, 7-up, or Ginger Ale.) Note: Please use this type of assortment every time soft drinks are ordered.	
Baltimore	Extension Family Life Specialists Break Existing set-up. Bring in buffet cart.	45 assorted soft drinks Sliced fresh fruit for 35 ppl. 35 ice cream bars	
Suite 1445/47	NCFR Finance Committee Meeting No set-up.	8 assorted soft drinks 4 assorted juices	
Chesapeake A	NCFR Focus Group Meeting Conference style for 15 ppl. Water pitcher & glasses on table. Wastebaskets. Bring food cart to room.	1/2 gallon coffee 1/2 gallon decaf	
Suite 1445/47	NCFR Executive Committee Meeting No set-up.	Check supply of soft drinks; add up to 6 assorted soft drinks and 4 assorted juices if needed.	

Sample Staging Guide

Program Requirement Sheet, November 10-15, 1993, File No. __

Session Times	Function and Set-up	AV	Food Required	Room
7:30 - 8:30 am (7 am set-up)	**CFLE Focus Group** Theater style to maximum capacity. Head table for 6 people. Table lectern. 1 deuce table at back of room for av equipment. Water station at back of room or in foyer.	BEO # ___		Annapolis
8:30 - 9:30 am (7:30 am set-up)	**First-Timers Reception** 4 serpentine serving tables against 2 side walls. 18 rounds of 10 people. Head table for 8 people. Table lectern. Water pitchers and glasses at each table. **See Diagram G.**	Microphone	BEO # ___	Harborview Room
9:45 - 11 am (8:45 am set-up)	**Opening Plenary Session** Theater style to capacity. Head table for 6 people on raised dais. Standing lectern next to head table. 1 section of raised dais at lower right section of Ballroom C for video camera. 1 deuce table at back of room for av equipment. Water stations at back of room or in foyer. **See Diagram H.**	Microphone 2 standing mikes in middle of room.		Ballroom C/D/E/F
11:45 am - 1 pm (9 am set-up)	**Poster Session I** 23 poster boards. Andrews/Bartlett Decorators will set. Set 1 schoolroom table by each poster board (see diagram). 2 - 3 water stations in the area. Leave this area as set until tear down at 12:15 pm, Mon., Nov. 15 (Andrews/Bartlett will take down poster boards). **See Diagram F.**			Ballroom A/B

APPENDIX H

Program at a Glance

STARTING TIMES	PLENARIES AND SPECIAL SESSIONS	SECTION AND STUDENT/NEW PROFESSIONAL SESSIONS	POSTERS AND ROUND TABLES	FOCUS GROUPS	NCFR BOARD, COMMITTEES, ASSN. OF COUNCILS	OTHER ORG.
7:30 am	Didactic Sem. - *The American Family Data Archive* (8 am)			CFLE; Nursing	94 Nominating Com.; AC/Public Policy Workshop	Groves Board Meeting
8:30 am	First Timers Reception			Fam. Ctrs.; Adoption		
9:45 am	Plenary - A. Billingsley					
11:00 am	Exhib. Grand Opening					
11:30 am	Burgess Award Add. Marie Peters Add.					
11:45 am	Public Policy Panel - *Family Impoverishment*	Symposia/Workshops/Papers I A Parent Education Model (EE) Family Caregiving (FH) Family-Religious Interaction (RF)	Posters I Adolescence and Childhood Cross-Cultural Issues Public Policy			
1:15 pm	RUP - *Families and Health*, W. Doherty	Symposia/Workshops/Papers II Moral Discourse, Eth. Min. Fams. & Soc. Constr. of Race/Ethn., Gender & Class Part I (EM) Effects of Commun. Viol. on Child. & Fams. (FP) Family Relations in China & Southeast Asia (IN) A Close Rel. Persp. on Dating & Mar. Rel. (RT)				
3:00 pm		Symposia/Workshops/Papers III Moral Discourse...Part II (EM) Impassioned Teaching (FF) Fam. Process & Chron. Illness: Concept. & Meth. Issues in Assess. African-Amer. Fams. (FH) Housing & Homelessness Among Families with Children (FP/RT) Adol. Issues: Sexuality, Pregnancy, Parenting (EE) The Lost Generation (FP) Family Science Issues (FS) Fams. in Context: Hist. & Cultur. Variations (RT)			AC Workshop - Small	
4:45 pm	Bus. Mtg/Mem. Forum					
6:15 pm	CFLE Reception	FP, RF, RT Sect. Bus. Mtgs.; S/NP Skills Exch.			Marie Peters Award Committee Mtg.	

129

APPENDIX I

Financial Impact Statement

Day	Original Room Block	Pre-reserved Day of Arrival	No Shows (Aver. 10%)	Single Rooms 37%	Double/Twin Rooms 63%	Suites	Total Room Revenue	Catering/Food and Beverage	Expresso	Palm Court (open for lunch and dinner)	Trader Vic's (open for lunch, dinner & cocktails)	Market Cafe (open for breakfast & lunch & dinner)	Cocktail Lounges	Room Service (Breakfast, Lunch, Dinner, Amenities and Hospitality Suites)
Wed. 11/7	0	7	0%	2	5	0	$00,000							
Thu. 11/8	50	104	7%	34	59	4	$00,000							
Fri. 11/9	200	289	9%	111	147	4	$00,000		$ 000	$0,000	$ 000	$ 0,000	Excellent to good traffic	$ 0,000
Sat. 11/10	350	463	7%	147	280	5	$00,000		$ 000	closed for lunch; $0,000 dinner	$ 000	$00,000	Very good traffic	$ 0,000
Sun. 11/11	400	498	8%	139	314	5	$00,000		$ 000	$0,000	$0,000	$00,000	Closed	$ 0,000
Mon. 11/12	400	484	11%	131	296	5	$00,000		$ 000	$0,000	$ 000	$00,000	Slow	$ 0,000
Tue. 11/13	300	332	14%	117	165	5	$00,000		$ 000	$0,000	$ 000	$ 0,000	Slow	$ 0,000
Wed. 11/14	10	52	15%	25	16	3	$00,000		$ 000	$0,000	$ 000	$0,000	Slow	$ 0,000
Totals	1710	2229	10%	706	1282	30	$000,000	$00,000.00	$0,000	$0,000	$0,000	$00,000		$00,000

Total Gross Revenue Sleeping Rooms, Food and Beverage/Catering, and Outlets = $000,000,000.00.
Total Room Nights used 2,018. Peak sleeping room night 458.

APPENDIX J

Meeting Planning Associations

American Society of Association Executives, 1575 Eye St. NW, Washington, DC 20005. Phone: 202-626-2764.

International Association of Conference Centers, 900 South Highway Drive, Fenton, MO 63026. Phone: 314-993-8575.

Meeting Planners International, 1950 Stemmons Freeway, Suite 5018, Dallas, TX 75207. Phone: 214-712-7700.

Professional Convention Management Association, 100 Vestavia Office Park, Suite 220, Birmingham, AL 35216. Phone 205-823-7262.

Religious Conference Management Association, One Hoosier Dome, Suite 120, Indianapolis, IN 46225.

APPENDIX K

Other Resources

Books and Guides

The Arranger: A Comfort Calculator. Published by Meeting Planners International, 1950 Stemmons Freeway, Dallas, TX 75207. Phone: 214-712-7700. MPI Members: $4.50. Nonmembers: $8.75.

The CLC Manual. (1989, 5th ed., edited by Bill Simmons). Published by the Convention Liaison Council, 1575 Eye St. NW, Suite 1200, Washington, DC 20005. Phone: 202-626-2764; fax: 202-371-8825. $22.95.

The Comprehensive Guide to Successful Conferences and Meetings. (1987, by J. Nadler, & Z. Nadler). Published by Jossey-Bass, 433 California St., San Francisco, CA 94104. Phone: 415-433-1767. $37.29 (includes postage and handling).

Convention Liaison Council Glossary. (1989). Published by the Convention Liaison Council, 1575 Eye St. NW, Suite 1200, Washington, DC 20005. Phone: 202-626-2764; fax: 202-371-8825. $9.95.

Fundamentals of Association Management. (1985, by S. H. Blackwell, P. R. Turner, & D. L. Wolfe). Published by the American Society of Association Executives, 1575 Eye Street NW, Washington, DC 20005. Phone: 202-626-2764.

The Guide to Campus & Non-Profit Meeting Facilities (5th Ed., edited by M. Nichols). Published by a division of AMARC, 2150 West 29th Ave., Suite 500, Denver, CO 80211. Phone: 303-433-1200. Lists over 385 college, university, and nonprofit conference centers in the United States and Canada. Free.

INFOLINE. (A series of practical guides, each devoted to a single subject). Published by the American Society for Training and Development, 1640 King St., Box 1443, Alexandria, VA 22313-2043. Phone: 703-683-8100; fax: 703-683-8103. $10 each book, plus shipping and handling. Entire set: $90, plus shipping and handling.

Getting the Most from Seminars and Conferences (1992)

Alternatives to Lecture (1986)

Create Effective Workshops (1986)

How to Create a Good Learning Environment (1985)

Succeed in Facilities Planning (1985)

How to Make a Large Group Presentation (1991)

Be a Better Speaker (1988)

How to Prepare and Use Effective Visual Aids (1984)

ADA: Impact on Training (1992)

ADA: Techniques for Accommodation (1992)

Make Every Presentation a Winner (1986)

How to Provide First-Rate Customer Service (1993)

Professional Meeting Management. (1989, edited by B. Nichols). Published by the Professional Convention Management Association, 100 Vestavia Office Park, Suite 220, Birmingham, AL 35216. Phone: 205-823-7262. Hardcover: $49.95 + $3.00 shipping and handling per copy.

Special Events, the Art and Science of Celebration. (1990, by J. J. Goldblatt). Published by Van Nostrand Reinhold, New York.

Periodicals

Association Meetings, published bimonthly in February, April, June, August, October, and December. Contact: The Laux Company, Inc., 63 Great Rd., Maynard, MA 01754. Phone 508-897-5552; Fax: 508-897-6824.

Business Travel News, published semimonthly in January, February, March, April, June, July, August; and bimonthly in May, September, October, November, and December. Contact: CMP Publications, Inc., 600 Community Dr., Manhasset, NY 11030. Phone: 516-562-5773; fax: 516-562-5407.

Convene, published by the Professional Convention Management Association, 100 Vestavia Office Park, Suite 220, Birmingham, AL 35216. Phone 205-823-7262; fax: 205-822-3891

Medical Meetings, published bimonthly with extra editions in spring and fall. Contact: The Laux Company, Inc., 63 Great Rd., Maynard, MA 01754. Phone: 508-897-5552; fax: 508-897-6824.

Meetings and Conventions, published monthly, two in March. Contact: Reed Travel Group, 500 Plaza Dr., Secaucus, NJ 07096. Phone: 303-388-4511 (subscriptions); fax: 201-319-1796.

Religious Conference Manager, published five times a year in March, June, August, October, and December. Contact: The Laux Company, Inc., 63 Great Rd., Maynard, MA 01754. Phone 508-897-5552; fax: 508-897-6824.

Successful Meetings, published monthly, except semimonthly in March. Contact: Bill Communications, Inc., 355 Park Ave. S., New York, NY 10010. Phone: 212-592-6400. $48 per year.

Music Licensing Agencies

American Society of Composers, Authors and Publishers (ASCAP), One Lincoln Plaza, New York, NY 10023. Phone: 1-800-627-9805; fax: 212-873-3133.

Broadcast Music Incorporated (BMI), Marketing Communications, 200 Schulz Dr., Red Bank, NJ 07701. Phone: 1-800-669-4BMI.

Continuing Education Units

Council on the Continuing Education Unit, 1101 Connecticut Ave. NW, Washington, DC 20036. Phone: 202-857-1122.

References

The CLC manual. (5th ed.). (1989). Washington, DC: Convention Liaison Council.

Conlin, J. (1993). Carnival of ideas. *Successful Meetings, 42*(2), 48-57.

Mitchell, D. (1985). How to publicize and promote your meeting. In S. H. Blackwell, P. R. Turner, & D. L. Wolfe (Eds.), *Fundamentals of association management* (pp. 246-271). Washington, DC: American Society of Association Executives.

Ramsborg, G. (1992). Making the most of committees. *Association Meetings, 44*(6), 61.

Seeley, J. H. (1985). Successful guidelines for evaluating your annual meeting. In S. H. Blackwell, P. R. Turner, & D. L. Wolfe (Eds.), *Fundamentals of association management* (pp. 215-236). Washington, DC: American Society of Association Executives.

Simmons, B. (Ed.). (1989a). Exhibits. In *The CLC manual* (5th ed., p. 94). Washington, DC: Convention Liaison Council.

Simmons, B. (Ed.). (1989b). Program planning. In *The CLC manual* (5th ed., pp. 34-37). Washington, DC: Convention Liaison Council.

Weiland, R. (1993). It's academic. *Successful Meetings, 42*(7), 50-52.

About the Author

Cynthia Winter, Certified Meeting Professional (CMP), is Conference Coordinator for the National Council on Family Relations (NCFR), Minneapolis, MN, a nonprofit, educational association. She is also Executive Coordinator (a volunteer position) for the Minnesota Christian Convention, a family convention with simultaneous programs for adults, children, and teens.

Conference planning has been a part of her job at NCFR from the beginning. This now full-time position has changed dramatically as the conference programs became more complex. She began working on-site at conferences in 1969. As conference needs changed, she updated herself professionally to meet the challenges. She has developed many materials for NCFR over the years to help in the conference planning process.

She regularly participates in training offered by meeting planning associations, including a 4-day hotel training course sponsored by the American Society of Association Executives. She has led two workshops at the Religious Conference Management Association and has been quoted several times in conference planning magazines. She has received awards from the Westin Hotel, Seattle, and the Marc Plaza Hotel, Milwaukee, for her expertise in conference planning.